WHAT'S THE BIG IDEA?

What's the Big Idea? ... and ideas around. In ... young people like you ... find most intriguing, ... The books in this serie... ...you need to know about the top-rate... ...

Books available now:
The Mind
Virtual Reality
Women's Rights
Animal Rights
The Environment
Time and the Universe
Nuclear Power
Genetics

Books coming soon:
Alien Life
The Paranormal
Food
The Media

We would love to hear what you think. If you would like to make any comments on this book or suggestions for future titles, please write to us at:

> What's the Big Idea?
> Hodder Children's Books
> 338 Euston Road
> London NW1 3BH

Text copyright © Anita Ganeri 1998

The right of Anita Ganeri to be identified as the author of the Work and the right of Christine Roche to be identified as the illustrator of the Work has been asserted by them in accordance with the Copyright, Designs and Patents Act 1988.

Illustrations copyright © Christine Roche 1998

Consultant: Alison Seaman, The National Society for Promoting Religious Education

Cover photograph courtesy of The Stock Market

Published by Hodder Children's Books 1998

10 9 8 7 6 5 4 3 2 1

All rights reserved. No part of this publication may be reproduced, stored in a retrieval system, or transmitted, in any form or by any means, without the prior written permission of the publisher, nor be otherwise circulated in any form of binding or cover other than that in which it is published and without a similar condition being imposed on the subsequent purchaser.

ISBN 0 340 66719 2

A Catalogue record for this book is available from the British Library.

Printed by Mackays of Chatham plc, Chatham, Kent

Hodder Children's Books
A division of Hodder Headline plc
338 Euston Road
London NW1 3BH

WHAT'S THE BIG IDEA?

Religion

Anita Ganeri
Illustrated by Christine Roche

Hodder Children's Books

a division of Hodder Headline plc

This book is for Susan and Andrew Malyan,
with love

A.G.

Contents

INTRODUCTION	6
What is religion?	8
How religion began	14
World religions	28
Why do we have religion?	58
Who is God?	64
A code for living	72
In religion's name	86
New religions	92
The challenge of science	100
The future of religion	108

INTRODUCTION

It's been around for a very long time. People live by it, swear by it, die for it and go to the ends of the Earth on its behalf. It's brought people together from all over the world and it's caused wars and conflict which have split families and communities apart. It's brought great hope, great joy and great compassion, as well as great prejudice and intolerance. And all of this in the name of ... RELIGION.

So what does religion mean to you?

- Going to the synagogue?

- Friday prayers at the mosque?

- Reading the Bible?

- Presents at Christmas?

- Eggs at Easter?

- Diwali fireworks?

Or does it mean much more to you than that? Do you think of yourself as religious? Maybe? Or is it simply something you learn at school? And if you do go to the church, or the mosque, or the synagogue, do you go because you want to or because your parents tell you to?

What is religion?

Here's what the dictionary says:

religion

1. Monastic condition; being a monk or a nun

2. One of the prevalent systems of faith and worship (e.g. Christianity, Islam etc.)

3. Human recognition of a superhuman controlling power and especially of a personal God entitled to obedience. The effect of such recognition on human conduct and mental attitude.

None the wiser? No one said it was going to be easy! The word "religion" is almost as mysterious as the phenomenon it describes. Nobody knows quite where it comes from. It may come from the Latin *religio* which means duty or reverence. Or it may come from *religare* which means to link or tie together.

There are many, many different views about what religion is. It means different things to different people.

Here are the views of some famous thinkers and teachers:

"There is only one religion though there are a hundred versions of it."

George Bernard Shaw (1856-1950)

"Religion...is the opium of the people."
Karl Marx (1818-1883)

"If God didn't exist, we would have invented him."
Albert Einstein (1879-1955)

"Religion is not what you will get after reading all the scriptures of the world. It is not really what is grasped by the brain. It is a heart grasp."
Mahatma Gandhi (1869-1948)

"Science investigates, religion interprets. Science gives man knowledge, religion gives man wisdom which is control."
Martin Luther King (1929-1968)

Reasons for Religion

Q: Why do people need religion?

A: From ancient times, people have felt the need for something "extra" in their lives, a **spiritual*** power or presence behind the physical reality of life, in order to give their lives purpose and meaning, and to make sense of the world around them. This presence is often called God. Belief in such a presence gives people hope, comfort and the strength to deal with life's problems and stresses and strains and celebrate life's joys. Organised religion, that is, people who share a common set of beliefs gathering together to worship, also gives people a set of rules, or code, for how to behave and live their lives.

* All the words printed in **bold** are explained in the glossary at the back of the book.

Q: What does religion do?

A: Religion helps to provide BIG answers to the BIG questions of life, the fundamental questions of human existence. Questions to which there are no certain answers. For example:

- Who am I?
- What am I?
- What is the meaning of life?
- What happens when I die?
- How was the world made?
- Why is there so much suffering in the world?
- Is there anybody out there?

Do you have answers to these questions?

Religions have a set of beliefs which try to provide the answers. But it is perfectly possible to have your own beliefs and not be religious. After all, everyone believes in something. And it is perfectly possible to ask the same questions but expect answers based not in religious belief but in science, or logic, or experience.

Living together

Britain is a melting pot for religions from across the world. In the 1950s and 1960s, for example, large numbers of Hindus, Muslims and Sikhs came to Britain from the Indian sub-continent, which had been part of the British Empire. They came mainly because they could not find jobs in their own countries, or because they did not agree with the political beliefs of their governments, and they brought their faith and beliefs with them. Today, you will find Hindu temples, Muslim mosques and Sikh gurdwaras in most big cities. Many second-generation Hindus, Muslims and Sikhs (who have been born and brought up in Britain) continue to follow their parents' religion, despite the differences they experience between home and school, or work.

For example, Hindus do not eat beef because they consider the cow to be a sacred animal. So a mega McDonald's beef-burger binge is well and truly out!

A multifaith society is one where people of many different religions are found.

Reading on...

This book looks mainly at the world's six major religions, which are practised worldwide by millions of people (approximate numbers given in brackets):

- HINDUISM (c. 732 million)
- JUDAISM (c. 17 million)
- BUDDHISM (c. 315 million)
- CHRISTIANITY (c. 3,000 million)
- ISLAM (c. 1,000 million)
- SIKHISM (c. 18 million)

But it also looks at smaller and lesser known religions, other views of life and some religions which are of historical interest only and are no longer practised. Of course, it cannot hope to cover everything - there are just too many points of view for that.

NB Dates are written as BCE (Before the Common Era) and CE (Common Era) instead of as BC (Before Christ) and AD (Anno Domini, or "in the year of the Lord"), as the latter are only appropriate for Christians and not for people of other religions.

FACT FLASH
There are about 5.75 billion people in the world. About 3.5 billion of them follow a religion.

How religion began

The French philosopher Auguste Comte (1798-1857) suggested that religion began as an attempt by ancient people to explain the workings of the natural world, long before they understood the science behind such phenomena as the weather, the changing seasons, and the movement of the Sun, Moon and planets.

Ancient people explained the world around them as the work of the gods who controlled nature, or by thinking that different aspects of nature actually were gods. For example in many religions the Sun was considered to be a god and many natural places, such as mountains and rivers, were worshipped as the homes of the gods, or as gods in their own right. Ancient people prayed to these gods and offered thanks for the Sun's heat and for life-giving rains which made their crops grow and enabled them to survive. People gathered to offer sacrifices to the gods, to please and appease them. If the gods were angry, a good harvest was by no means guaranteed.

From these early gatherings, the idea of organised religion began to grow, as people from various groups and tribes began to share their religious beliefs and rituals (more about these on page 82). Soon people started to question their own place in the world, their relationship with the gods, and to search for deeper meaning to their lives.

Did cave people believe in God?

Quite possibly! In the Lascaux Caves, in south-west France, the walls are covered with pictures of almost 600 animals, including mammoths, bison and four giant white bulls. These were drawn some 17,000 years ago by Ice Age artists. Some experts think that these prehistoric Picassos painted the animals they hunted for food and skins in order to gain some sort of magic or spiritual power over them and ensure successful hunting in the future. Other similar paintings, but even older, have been found deep in caves in Spain, Africa and Australia.

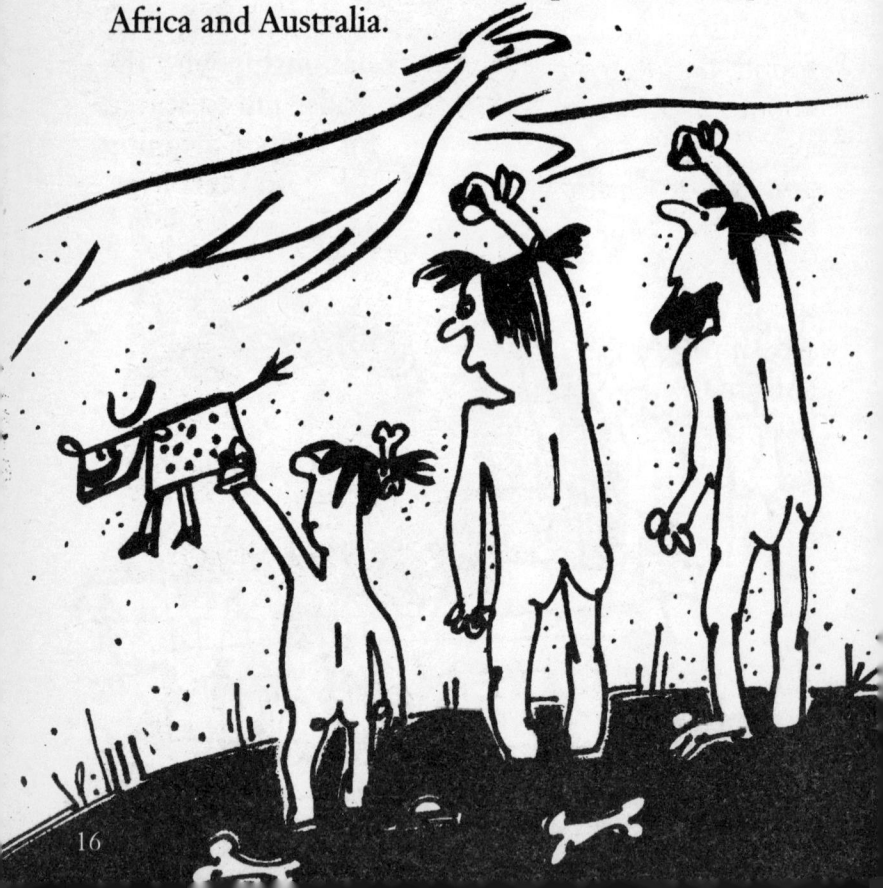

Even earlier clues exist to suggest that prehistoric people had some form of religious beliefs. Neanderthal people, living 80,000 to 40,000 years ago, had funeral ceremonies for their dead. At one burial site found in Iraq, a child was laid to rest surrounded by flowers, a now traditional way of paying your last respects.

Small statues, carved from stone or mammoth ivory, have also been found, dating from about 22,000 years ago. They show female figures and heads, suggesting that people might have worshipped a mother goddess of some type.

MOTHER GODDESS

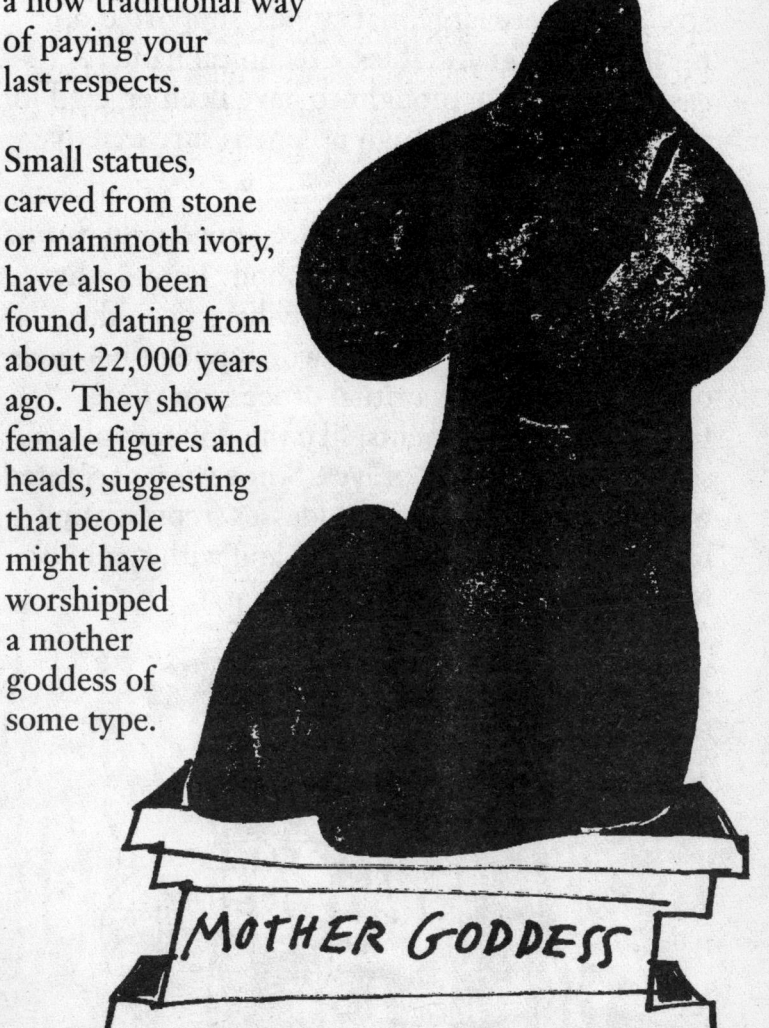

Down in the dolmens

From prehistoric caves, the places people chose as sites of worship gradually became more elaborate. Between 4-6,000 years ago, structures made up of large stones, called *megaliths*, were erected all over Europe. Some stones stood on their own. Other structures were large, flat stones, supported on uprights, like giant tables. (Technical name: a *dolmen*.) Both are thought to have been erected for religious reasons, though no one is sure exactly what these were.

At Carnac in France, you can see row upon row of standing stones. Even now, nobody knows why they were put there. They may have been the place where ancient people worshipped their gods, or have marked out a ritual procession route. Other stone monuments, like the dolmens above, served as shrines and graves. Some were decorated with pictures of mother goddesses (representing birth and the start of new life) and with symbols for the Sun, Moon, Earth and Water.

Stairway to heaven

The Mesopotamians, who lived in ancient Iraq some 5,000 years ago went a stage further in honouring the gods. They built huge, stepped pyramid-like towers, called *ziggurats*. At the top was a temple where priests offered food and drinks to the gods, and sang of their great deeds. All of this was crucial for keeping the gods happy. The Mesopotamians believed that the gods controlled everything that happened in the world. If they were neglected, they might get angry and send floods, plagues and pestilence as punishment. The chief gods of Mesopotamia were Enlil, Lord of the Wind, and Anu, his father, who was Lord of Heaven.

The stepped sides of the ziggurat were seen as stairs for the gods to come down to Earth and for the faithful to climb up to Heaven. The shape of the ziggurat represented a legendary cosmic mountain which bridged the gap between Heaven and Earth.

The afterlife in Ancient Egypt

The Ancient Egyptians (c. 3000-30 BCE) were firm believers in life after death and made elaborate preparations for it. They believed that each person had three **souls** - the *ka*, *ba* and *akh*. For these to flourish in the next world, the dead person's body had to be preserved from decay. And the best way to do this? MUMMIFICATION, of course!

The body was taken to the "Beautiful House", the embalmer's workshop. The brain and other organs were removed, and the body packed in natron salt to dry it out. It was then padded with linen and sawdust, to make it look more life-like, oiled and wrapped in bandages, with amulets and charms tucked in between. Then it was put in a coffin and placed in a tomb. The pharaohs were buried first in pyramids, and later in rock-cut tombs. (Things weren't so great if you were poor. Then a hole in the hot sand had to do.)

CATS WERE MUMMIFIED

AND SO WERE OTHER ANIMALS!

With your body safely preserved, your soul could start its journey to the next world. First you had to undergo a series of trials. The final one took place in the Judgement Hall of Osiris, god of the dead. Here your heart was weighed against the Feather of Truth. If you'd led a sinful life, your heart would be heavy and tip the scales. You were then fed to a hideous monster. If you'd led a virtuous life, your heart and the feather balanced out. You could then travel on to paradise in the Kingdom of the West.

Anubis was the god of mummification.

Greek gods and Roman religion

The Ancient Greeks (c. 750-30 BCE) believed that earthly events were controlled by the great gods of Mount Olympus. Zeus was the king of the gods. Although the gods were **immortal** and all-powerful, they showed many human qualities. They got angry, fell in and out of love, had quarrels, made up, and so on.

When the Romans conquered Greece from the 2nd century BCE, they adopted many of the Greek gods and goddesses as their own and matched up their existing gods with suitable Greek ones. A quick change of name and Neptune was your uncle. The Romans also worshipped their own family spirits - the lares, penates and manes. Every Roman home had them.

MEET THE GODS

1. Zeus   Roman: Jupiter
Status: King of the gods; god of storms.

2. Hera   Roman: Juno
Status: Queen of the gods; god of women and marriage. Wife of Zeus.

3. Poseidon   Roman: Neptune
Status: God of the sea and of earthquakes. Brother of Zeus.

4. Hestia   Roman: Vesta
Status: Goddess of the hearth. Gave up her place on Olympus to Dionysus. Sister of Zeus.

5. Pluto   Roman: Dis
Status: God of the dead and of the underworld. Brother of Zeus.

6. Demeter   Roman: Ceres
Status: Goddess of plants and crops.

7. Aphrodite   Roman: Venus
Status: Goddess of love and beauty.

8. Hephaestos   Roman: Vulcan
Status: God of craftsmen and of smiths.

9. Ares   Roman: Mars
Status: God of war.

10. Artemis   Roman: Diana
Status: Goddess of hunting and of the Moon.

11. Apollo   Roman: Apollo
Status: God of the Sun, light, music and the truth. Twin brother of Artemis.

12. Hermes   Roman: Mercury
Status: Messenger of the gods. God of travellers and thieves.

13. Athene   Roman: Minerva
Status: Goddess of war, wisdom and Athens.

14. Dionysus   Roman: Bacchus
Status: God of wine and the theatre. Replaced Hestia.

Viking world view

The Vikings flourished in northern Europe from the 8th-11th centuries CE. They were superb sailors, intrepid explorers and fierce warriors. They were also great poets and storytellers, telling long, complex tales about the exploits of their gods. To explain how the world began, they told this story:

Before the world was made, there was a place of ice in the North, called Niflheim, and a place of fire in the South, called Muspell. Between the two lay a great void, called Gunnungagap. Eleven rivers flowed from Niflheim, froze and plugged the gap. And as the ice reached Muspell, it melted in the heat. From the melting drops two creatures were formed - the Frost Giant, Ymir, and a huge cow, Audumla. From Ymir's sweat came more Frost Giants.

One day, a man appeared. This was Buri who had a son, called Bor. Bor married a Frost Giantess, called Bestla, and had three sons - Odin, Vili and Ve, the first gods. They hated the evil Frost Giants, killed Ymir and dragged his body into Gunnungagap where it formed the world. His flesh became the earth; his teeth and bones the rocks and mountains; his blood filled the seas and rivers. His skull became the arch of the sky and his brains the clouds. Sparks of fire from Muspell became the Sun, Moon and stars.

The first humans were made from the roots of two trees - an ash and an elm. The ash became Ask, the first man, and the elm became Embla, the first woman.

And that was how the world was made.

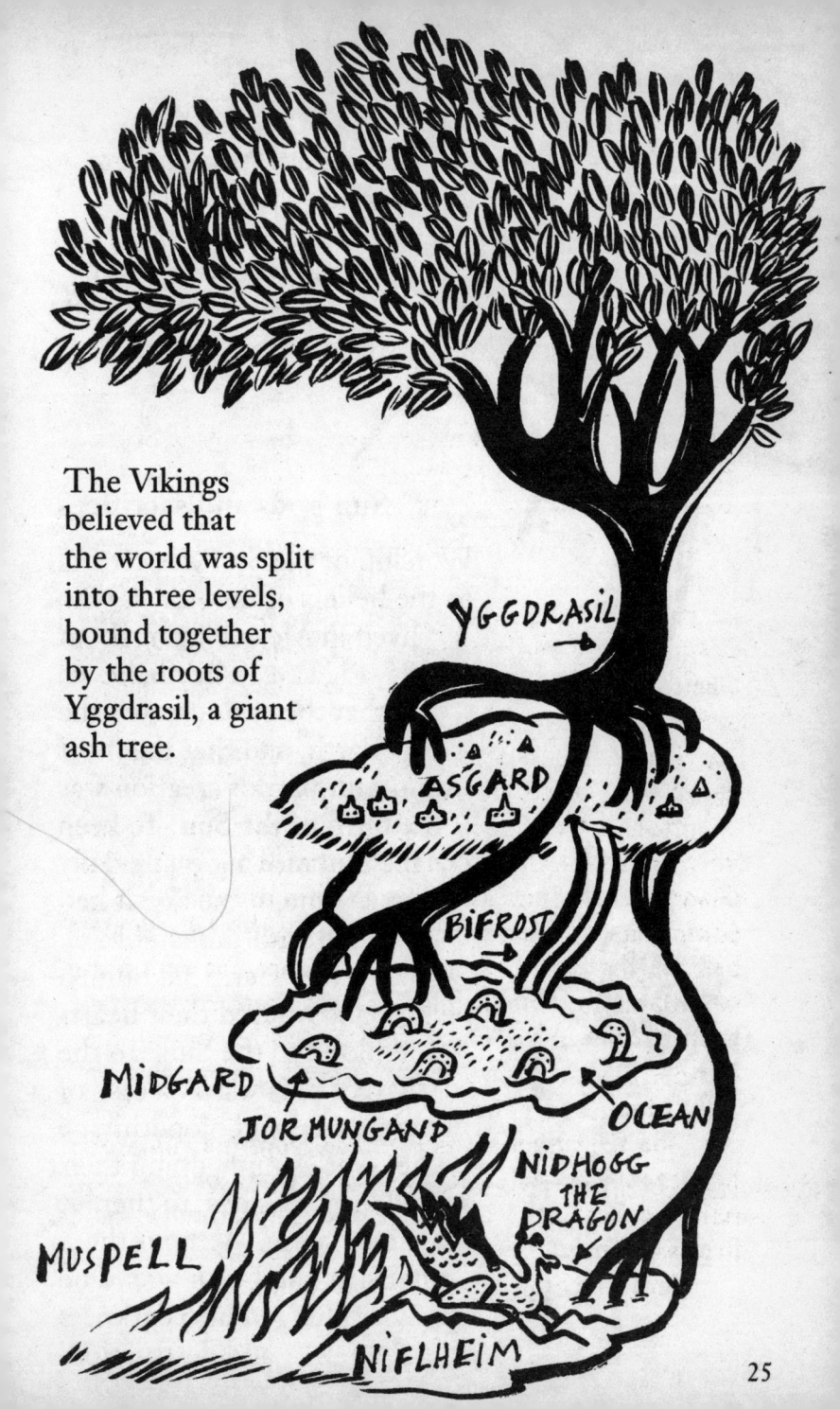

The Vikings believed that the world was split into three levels, bound together by the roots of Yggdrasil, a giant ash tree.

Sun gods and sacrifices

Worship of the Sun was central to the beliefs of the Aztecs who lived in Mexico from about 1325-1521 CE. They believed that the gods created the Earth, and that the most important part of creation was the birth of the Sun. To keep the Sun moving on its daily course through the sky, it had to be fed with human blood. So the Aztecs sacrificed human beings, and offered their hearts and blood to the Sun. To the Aztecs, this wasn't a case of being brutal and bloodthirsty. They were simply doing their sacred duty. Besides, to them it made sense. Without these offerings, the Earth would be plunged into darkness and destruction.

The Aztecs believed that they lived in the world of the "fifth sun". At the end of this era, the world would end violently unless they performed human sacrifices to the gods.

Sacrifices took place in front of the huge stone temples built to honour the gods, during special ceremonies throughout the year. The victims were usually prisoners of war - men, women and children. Their hearts were cut out, their bodies thrown down the temple steps and their skulls stuck on huge skull racks for all to see. Gruesome, but for the Aztecs a very honourable way to go!

Unlike those that are described above, the religions that follow are still practised today.

Spirit worship

In parts of the world, such as Africa, North and South America, and Australasia, people who live close to nature, relying on it for food and survival, have traditionally practised spirit religions, based on the worship of spirits believed to live in trees, animals, and other features of the natural landscape. These beliefs are a way of showing a mixture of reverence, fear and respect for the natural world. In many places, these spirit religions have now died out. But some remain.

For the rainforest people of South America, the most powerful animal spirit is that of the mighty jaguar, revered for its strength and its hunting prowess. To visit the spirit world, the tribe's **shaman**, or witch doctor, is believed to be able to transform himself into a jaguar. Dressed in a jaguar skin and a necklace of jaguar teeth, he falls into a deep trance in order to ask favours of the spirits, such as better hunting or a cure from sickness.

OR A CURE FOR SICKNESS

For the Aborigines of Australia, the land is sacred and must be looked after. They believe it was created thousands of years ago, in a period called the Dreamtime. The spirits of their ancestors travelled across Australia, some in human form, some as animals, shaping the landscape as they went. The most sacred Aborigine site is *Uluru* (Ayers Rock). Legend says that the rock was created by two boys playing in the mud and rain, during the Dreamtime.

> *"We return thanks to our mother, the Earth, which sustains us...to the wind, which moving the air has banished diseases...to the Sun, that he has looked upon the Earth with a beneficent eye."*
> (Native American prayer)

HINDUISM

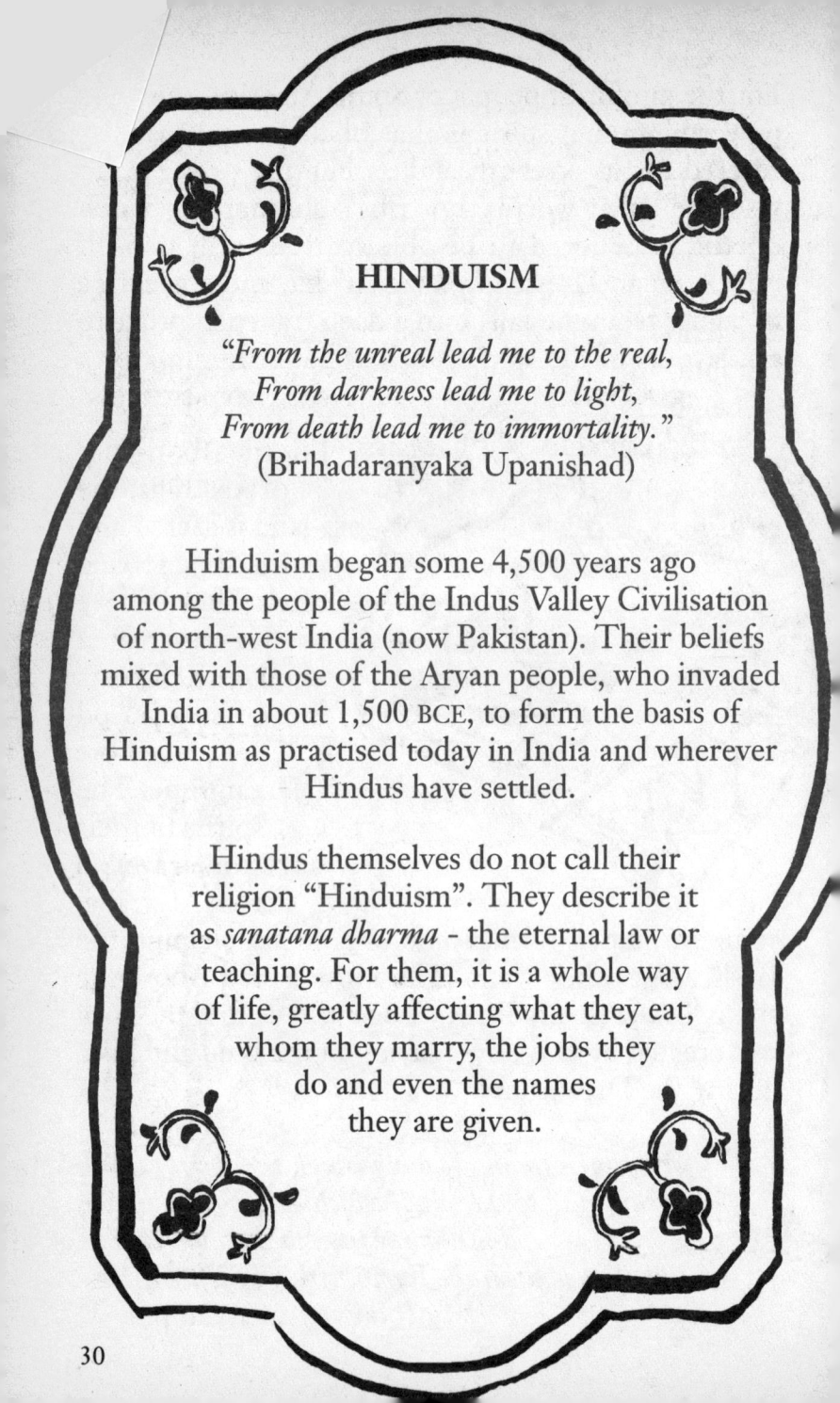

*"From the unreal lead me to the real,
From darkness lead me to light,
From death lead me to immortality."*
(Brihadaranyaka Upanishad)

Hinduism began some 4,500 years ago among the people of the Indus Valley Civilisation of north-west India (now Pakistan). Their beliefs mixed with those of the Aryan people, who invaded India in about 1,500 BCE, to form the basis of Hinduism as practised today in India and wherever Hindus have settled.

Hindus themselves do not call their religion "Hinduism". They describe it as *sanatana dharma* - the eternal law or teaching. For them, it is a whole way of life, greatly affecting what they eat, whom they marry, the jobs they do and even the names they are given.

It is also an immensely practical and flexible religion, with many different ways of believing and worshipping. Despite this, most Hindus share the same basic beliefs. They believe in a supreme soul or spirit, an ultimate reality which underlies everything. They call this great soul *Brahman*. Legend says that a wise man taught his son about Brahman by sprinkling some salt in some water. Then he told his son to take the salt out. Of course he couldn't - it had dissolved. The wise man compared it to Brahman's presence in the world - invisible but in everything.

YOU SEE, THIS IS LIKE BRAHMAN'S PRESENCE IN THE WORLD - INVISIBLE BUT IN EVERYTHING.

Each individual person also has an individual soul, called *Atman*.

Hindus believe that when you die, your soul is reborn in another body. This is called **reincarnation**. The aim of a Hindu's life is to break free of the endless cycle of birth, death and rebirth and to achieve *moksha*, when your individual soul becomes one with Brahman. How you are reborn depends on how you act in each life. This is called **karma** - the law of cause and effect. If you lead a good life, you will have a higher rebirth, closer to moksha. If you lead a bad life, you will be born lower down, and further away from moksha.

Hindus worship many different gods and goddesses, representing different aspects of Brahman's nature and power. The three main gods are Brahma (the creator), Vishnu (the protector) and Shiva (the destroyer). Two of the most popular of all the gods are Rama and Krishna. Both are **avatars**, or appearances of Vishnu, sent to Earth to save the world from disaster.

IF YOU DON'T BEHAVE YOU'LL COME BACK AS A COCKROACH!

EVEN COCKROACHE GET ANOTH CHANCE.

BRAHMA    **VISHNU**    **SHIVA**

The gods are worshipped in temples, called *mandirs*, or in shrines at home, by the roadside or out in the fields. Some Hindus worship several gods. Some worship only one; and some worship none at all.

"Religion is not in doctrines, in dogmas, nor in intellectual arguments. It is being and becoming. It is realisation."
(Swami Vivekananda 1863-1902, Indian holy man)

- **Fact File**
Numbers of Hindus: c. 732 million
Where began: India/Pakistan (c. 2,500 BCE)
Places of worship: mandirs (temples); shrines at home
Sacred texts: *Vedas; Upanishads; Ramayana; Mahabharata* (especially the *Bhagavad Gita*)
Major festivals: Holi; Diwali

JUDAISM

"And Moses wrote all the words of the Lord... And he took the book of the covenant, and read it to the people. And they said, All that the Lord has said, we will do, and be obedient." (Exodus 24)

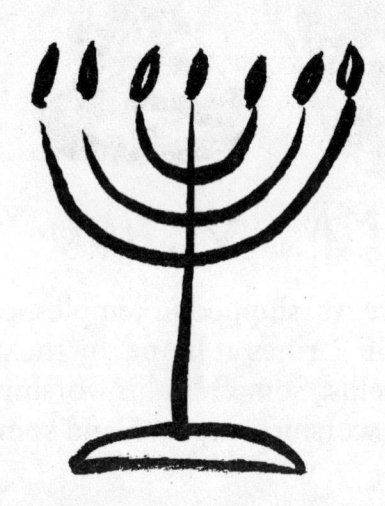

The Jewish religion began about 4,000 years ago in the Middle East. According to Jewish scriptures, the first Jew was Abraham, a member of a nomadic tribe, the Hebrews. He taught people to worship one God only, who created the world and everything in it. He also entered into a covenant (agreement) with God; Abraham's descendants would worship God and they would become God's Chosen People and live in the Promised Land of Canaan (now Israel).

Today, there are about 17 million Jews living in Israel and all over the world. Anyone whose mother is Jewish counts as a Jew, whether they follow Jewish religious practices or not.

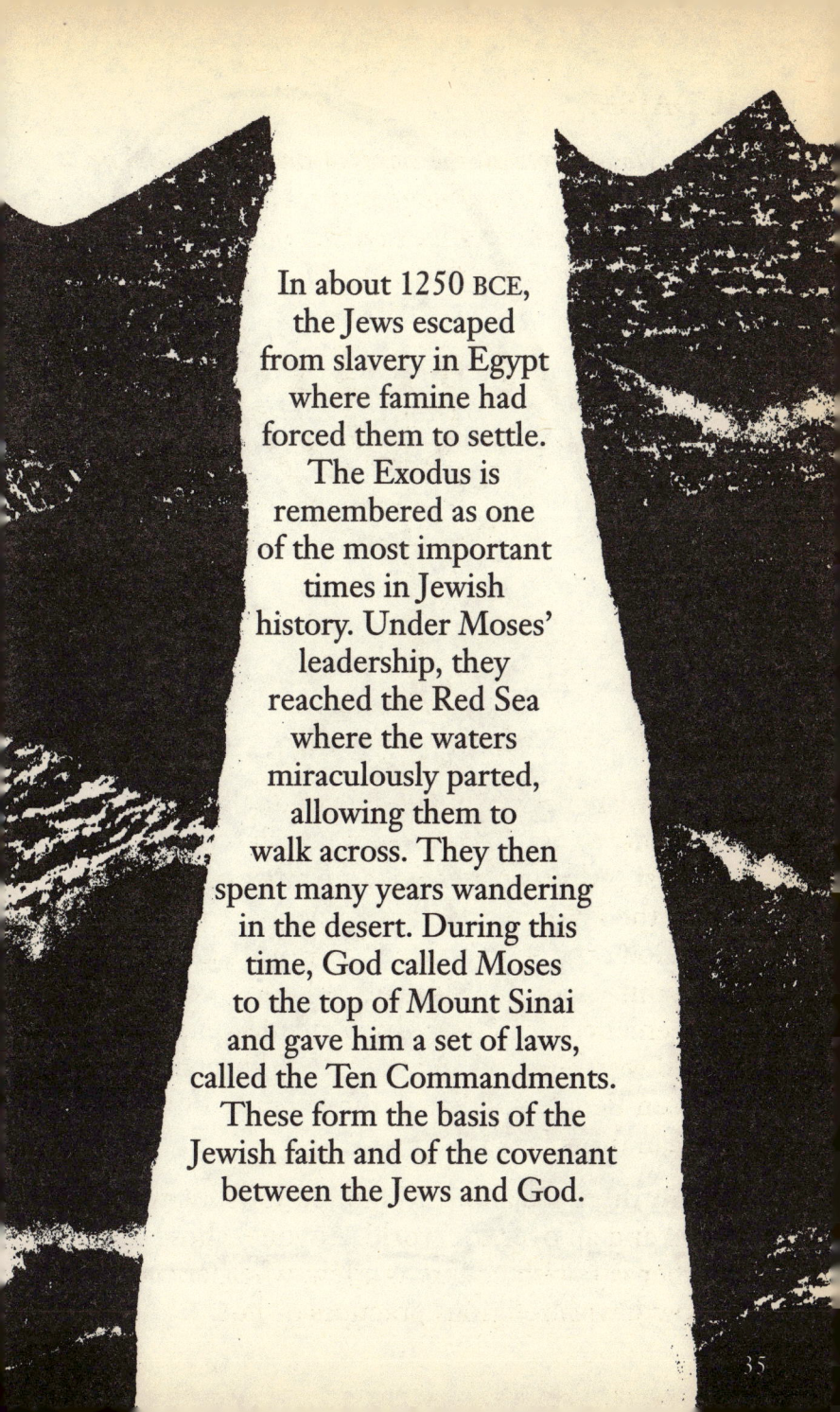

In about 1250 BCE, the Jews escaped from slavery in Egypt where famine had forced them to settle. The Exodus is remembered as one of the most important times in Jewish history. Under Moses' leadership, they reached the Red Sea where the waters miraculously parted, allowing them to walk across. They then spent many years wandering in the desert. During this time, God called Moses to the top of Mount Sinai and gave him a set of laws, called the Ten Commandments. These form the basis of the Jewish faith and of the covenant between the Jews and God.

The Ten Commandments

1. I am the Lord your God. Worship no other God but me.
2. Do not make images to worship.
3. Do not take my name in vain.
4. Keep the Sabbath day holy.
5. Respect your father and mother.
6. Do not kill.
7. Do not commit adultery.
8. Do not steal.
9. Do not tell lies about other people.
10. Do not be envious of other people's possessions.

Throughout their history, the Jews have suffered **persecution** because of their culture and religious beliefs. This reached its worst excesses during World War II when some six million Jews (out of a total of ten million) were murdered by the German Nazis. This horrific event became known as the Holocaust. In 1948, the modern state of Israel was founded as a homeland for Jews from all over the world.

• Fact File
Numbers of Jews: c. 17 million
Where began: the Middle East (c.2000 BCE)
Places of worship: synagogues
Sacred texts: *Tenakh* (Hebrew Bible); *Torah* (first five books of the Tenakh); *Talmud*
Major festivals: Rosh Hashanah; Yom Kippur; Pesach; Sukkot; Shavuot

BUDDHISM

"The person who goes to the Buddha for refuge... he goes indeed to a great refuge. Then he sees the four great truths: sorrow, the cause of sorrow, the end of sorrow, and the path of eight stages which leads to the end of sorrow."
(The Dhammapada)

Buddhists follow the teachings of a nobleman, Siddhartha Gautama, born in Nepal about 2,500 years ago. Gautama grew up in luxury in his father's palace, shielded from the troubles of daily life. One day, he left the palace secretly, on a journey which changed his life. First he saw an old man, then a sick man, then a dead man. Life was full of such suffering, he was told. Then he saw a monk, content with his lot, despite having no worldly possessions. Gautama decided to follow his example.

He left the palace for ever and spent many years fasting and praying, in his quest to find an answer to suffering. While meditating under a bodhi (fig) tree in Bodh Gaya, India, he at last saw the true meaning of life unfold. It was like waking from a dream. He became the Buddha, the enlightened one.

The Buddha spent the rest of his life travelling around India as a wandering monk. His message was that people suffered because they always wanted what they could not have. But there was a way out of suffering, if they followed his teaching.

- **The Four Noble Truths**
1. All human life involves suffering.
2. The cause of suffering is greed and desire.
3. Suffering can be overcome.
4. The way to overcome suffering is to follow the Noble Eightfold Path, a Middle Path between extreme luxury and hardship.

• The Noble Eightfold Path

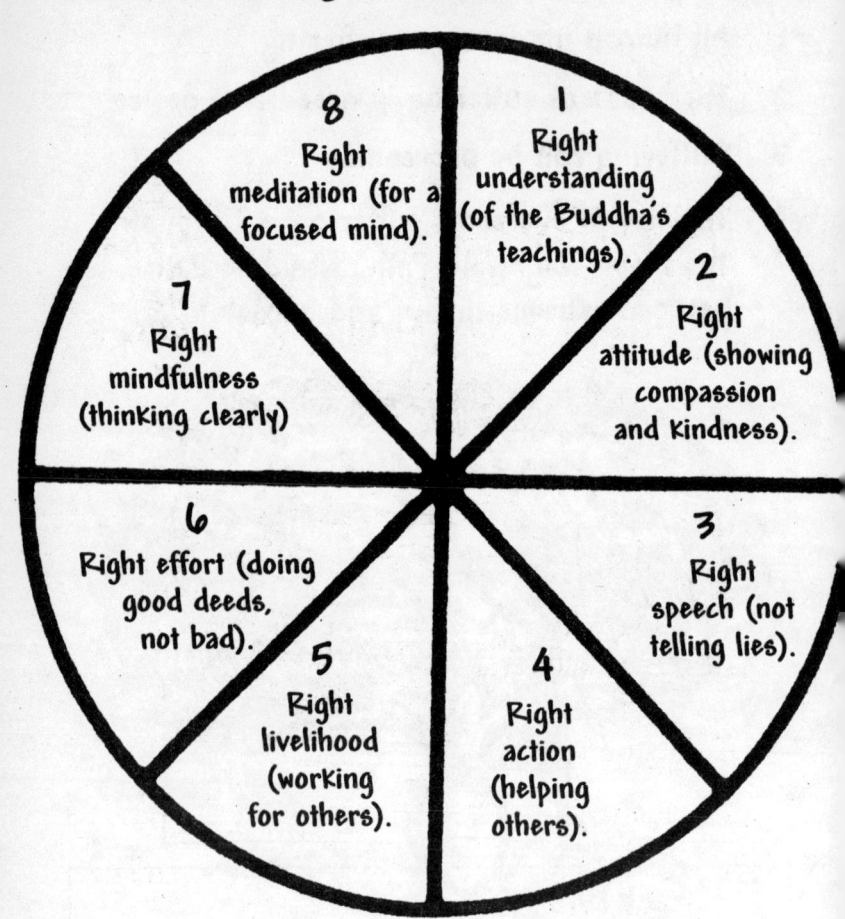

1. Right understanding (of the Buddha's teachings).
2. Right attitude (showing compassion and kindness).
3. Right speech (not telling lies).
4. Right action (helping others).
5. Right livelihood (working for others).
6. Right effort (doing good deeds, not bad).
7. Right mindfulness (thinking clearly).
8. Right meditation (for a focused mind).

The Three Jewels

Buddhists commit themselves to three things: the Buddha; the *dharma* (his teaching) and the *sangha* (the community of Buddhist laypeople, monks and nuns). These are called the Three Jewels because they are so precious. The Buddha is often described as a doctor, the dharma as medicine, and the sangha as the nurse who administers the medicine to the sick.

*"Not to do evil,
To cultivate good,
To purify one's mind:
This is the teaching of the Buddhas."*
(The Dhammapada)

THE BUDDHA IS OFTEN DESCRIBED AS A DOCTOR... THE DHARMA AS MEDICINE... AND THE SANGHA AS THE NURSE.

- **Fact File**

Numbers of Buddhists: c. 315 million
Where began: Nepal/India (6th century BCE)
Places of worship: stupas (shrines); viharas (monasteries)
Sacred texts: *Tipitaka* (the Three Baskets), the *Dhammapada* (sayings of the Buddha); the *Diamond Sutra* and others
Major festivals: Wesak (Buddha's birth, enlightenment and death)

JAINISM

The Jain religion was founded in India in the 6th century BCE, by Mahavira, a contemporary of the Buddha. Born into a wealthy Hindu warrior family, he left home at the age of thirty to become a monk. He is believed to be the twenty-fourth and last in line of great spiritual teachers, called *Tirthankaras*, or "path-makers". Jain temples contain statues of all twenty-four teachers.

Like Buddhists and Hindus, Jains believe in karma and reincarnation. They believe that, by following the guidelines of "right faith, right conduct and right knowledge", they can seek release from the cycle of life, death and rebirth. Those who achieve release are called *jinas*, or conquerors. Another central belief is in *ahimsa*, or non-violence. Jains do not believe in harming any living thing and are strict vegetarians. Some even wear masks to avoid swallowing insects.

Today, there are about 3.8 million Jains, mostly living in western India where their religion began.

"I ask pardon of all living creatures.
May all of them pardon me.
May I have a friendly relationship with
all beings and unfriendly with none."
(Jain prayer)

ZOROASTRIANISM

Founded in ancient Persia (now Iran) more than 3,000 years ago, by a prophet called Zoroaster (or Zarathustra), Zoroastrian belief centres on the struggle between good, represented by God (*Ahura Mazda*), and evil, which comes from the Destructive Spirit (*Angra Mainyu*). When people die, they are judged by their behaviour. Virtuous people will pass over a bridge to Heaven. Sinful people will fall off the bridge and plummet down to Hell.

The worship of the sacred fire, representing truth and righteousness, lies at the centre of Zoroastrian worship. And because fire is sacred, dead bodies cannot be cremated. Nor can they be buried because this would pollute the Earth. So they are placed in "Towers of Silence" for birds of prey to devour.

Today, there are about 100,000 Zoroastrians. Many now live in India where they are known as *Parsis* ("Persians") because of their Persian origins.

"This I ask thee, tell me truly Lord.
Who in the beginning, at creation, was the father of order?
Who established the course of Sun and stars?
Through whom does the Moon wax, then wane?
This and yet more, O Mazda, I seek to know."
(Zoroastrian hymn)

TWO CHINESE RELIGIONS

In the 6th century BCE, two great philosophers and religious teachers emerged in China - Confucius and Lao Tzu. Both founded systems of beliefs which are still practised in China today.

Confucius (K'ung Fu-tzu) was born in 551 BCE. He lived in a time of growing social disorder in China, with frequent wars between rival rulers. Dismayed by what he saw, particularly by what he saw as a breakdown in traditional family values, he gave up his government post in order to teach the best way to live in the world. Confucius believed that a perfect society was possible if people showed respect for others, honoured their ancestors and followed the five virtues of kindness, righteousness, sobriety, wisdom and trustworthiness.

The sayings for which Confucius was famous were originally used as official government texts, consulted by China's rulers when they needed advice. They were so influential that, right up to the beginning of this century, China's civil service exams were based on them.

CONFUCIUS SAYS: A GOOD PERSON ALWAYS SEEKS TO HELP OTHERS TO DO GOOD - NOT TO DO ILL -.

CONFUCIUS SAYS: UNTIL YOU KNOW ABOUT LIFE HOW CAN YOU KNOW ABOUT DEATH.

Lao Tzu was an eminent sage and philosopher, credited with founding Taoism. The *Tao*, or "Way", refers to the ultimate spiritual force which underlies everything in the world. The aim of a Taoist's life is to seek to become one with the Tao, and so achieve liberation and become an Immortal.

According to legend, Lao Tzu left his job in charge of the state archives, and set off for the mountains on ox-back. The soldier guarding the mountain pass asked him to write down his teachings. These writings became the *Tao Te Ching*, the sacred book of Taoism.

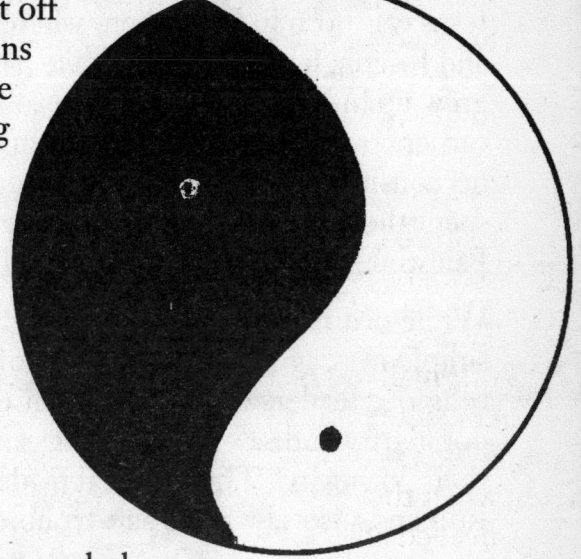

The yin and yang symbol represents the male (yang) and female (yin) forces which shape everything in the universe. Harmony between these two forces is vitally important in Taoist thought.

"He that knoweth, nothing sayeth.
He that sayeth, nothing knoweth."
(Lao Tzu)

CHRISTIANITY

"I am the light of the world. Whoever follows me will have the light of life and will never walk in darkness." (Gospel of St John)

Christianity is based on the teachings of a man called Jesus, who lived in Palestine (now Israel) 2,000 years ago. His followers gave him the title of Christ, the anointed one or Messiah.

Jesus was born in Bethlehem where his parents, Mary and Joseph, had travelled to take part in a census. He grew up in Nazareth where he probably trained as a carpenter. At the age of thirty, Jesus was baptised by his cousin, John, and a new life began for him. He spent the next three years travelling around Palestine, preaching, teaching and healing the sick.

While ordinary people flocked to hear Jesus's simple message about the power of God's love, the religious leaders of Jerusalem felt threatened by his popularity and saw his teachings as a challenge to their authority. The political leaders of the city, the Romans, also saw Jesus as a troublemaker.

He was arrested, while in Jerusalem for the feast of Passover, charged with **blasphemy** and sentenced to death by being crucified on a cross.

Three days after the crucifixion, according to scriptures, Jesus's tomb was found to be empty. Over the next forty days, he appeared several times to his disciples. Then he ascended, or rose, into heaven, to be reunited with God.

Christians believe that God became human in Jesus so they call him Son of God. He came down to Earth to save people from their sins and teach them about God's love and forgiveness . He did this by sacrificing his own life. Christians believe in one God, but in three aspects - as the Father (the creator of the world), as the Son (Jesus) and as the Holy Spirit (the power and presence of God in the world).

The Prodigal Son

Jesus often taught in stories, called parables. The following parable shows the importance of forgiveness.

"For God so loved the world,
that he gave his only son,
that whosoever believes in him should not perish
but have everlasting life."
(Gospel of St John)

> • **Fact file**
> **Numbers of Christians:** c. 3,000 million
> **Where began:** the Middle East (1st century CE)
> **Places of worship:** churches; cathedrals; chapels
> **Sacred texts:** *The Bible* (Old and New Testaments)
> **Major festivals:** Easter; Christmas

ISLAM

Al-Fatihah (The Opener) from the Qur'an

*In the name of Allah, Most Gracious, Most Merciful.
Praise be to Allah, Lord of the worlds,
The Most Gracious, the Most Merciful:
Master of the Day of Judgement.
You alone we worship and You alone we ask for help.
Guide us on the straight way, the way of those You
have favoured,
Not the path of those who earn Your anger, nor of those
who go astray.*

THE WORD 'ISLAM' MEANS SUBMISSION OR OBEDIENCE TO ALLAH, OR GOD.

Followers of Islam are called *Muslims*, or obedient ones. They believe that Allah's wishes for the world were revealed through a series of prophets, the last of whom, Muhammad, was born in Makkah (Mecca, now in Saudi Arabia) in about 570 CE.

Even though he was a successful merchant, Muhammad felt dissatisfied with life and spent much of his time in solitary prayer and contemplation in the mountains. One night, as he lay asleep in a cave on Mount Hira, the angel Jibril appeared to him and began to reveal Allah's message to him. More revelations followed throughout Muhammad's life. Muhammad returned to Makkah and began to teach people that they should worship only Allah, the one true God.

The holy book of Islam is called the *Qur'an*, or recitation. It is believed to contain the actual words of Allah, as revealed to Muhammad by the angel Jibril. It gives Allah's guidance on every aspect of life for people everywhere. Muhammad himself could not read or write but each year, during the month of Ramadan, he recited it to make sure he had remembered everything perfectly. Later, his followers wrote down parts of the *Qur'an* on scraps of paper and palm leaves. These were collected together in book form in the 630s CE and have remained unchanged to this day.

Five observances of faith, called the *Five Pillars of Islam*, form the basis of Islam.

1. *Shahadah*, or statement of faith: "There is no god but Allah and Muhammad is the messenger of Allah".

2. *Salah*, or prayer. Muslims must pray five times a day. Prayers are said in Arabic. Muslims must face the holy city of Makkah to pray.

3. *Zakah*, or giving alms. Every year, Muslims should give part of their wealth to the poor and needy.

GOOD CHARACTER MELTS AWAY MISTAKES JUST AS WATER MELTS AWAY ICE. BAD CHARACTER SPOILS DEEDS JUST AS VINEGAR SPOILS HONEY.

4. *Sawm*, or fasting. Muslims are required to fast from just before dawn until sunset during the holy month of Ramadan. This helps to teach discipline and self-control.

5. *Hajj*, or **pilgrimage**. Every Muslim has to make a pilgrimage to Makkah at least once in their lives, if he or she has the health and wealth.

> • **Fact file**
> **Numbers of Muslims:** c. 1,000 million
> **Where began:** Saudi Arabia
> **Places of worship:** mosques
> **Sacred texts:** *The Qur'an*
> **Major festivals:** Id-ul-Fitr; Id-ul-Adha

RELIGION IN JAPAN

"Turn to the kami in times of need."
(Shinto proverb)

Shinto, which means the "way of the gods", is an ancient Japanese religion, still practised by about five million people. It is based around the worship of spirits, called *kami*, believed to live in plants and animals, mountains, rivers and trees, and everywhere in the natural world.

The most important kami is the Sun goddess, *Amaterasu-Omikami*, also worshipped as the ancestor of the Japanese emperors. Legend tells how, one day, Amaterasu-Omikami quarrelled with her brother, the storm god Susanoo. She was so terrified of his terrible temper, she went to hide in a cave. And as she hid, the world was plunged into darkness and chaos. The other gods had to act quickly to restore light and order. Outside the cave, they laughed and danced until curiosity got the better of Amaterasu-Omikami and she emerged from the cave to get a better look.

Many Japanese people practise a mixture of Shinto and Buddhism. It is quite usual, for example, to have a Shinto wedding and a Buddhist funeral. The two main strands of Japanese Buddhism are *Zen* and *Pure Land*, both of which came to Japan in about the 13th century CE.

Followers of Pure Land Buddhism worship *Amitabha*, the Buddha of Infinite Light. He is Lord of the Pure Land, a beautiful, peaceful paradise. Anyone who calls his name when they die will be reborn in the Pure Land.

Zen means meditation, seen as the best way to achieve enlightenment. Zen Buddhists have many ways to help them meditate. One involves asking riddles, such as: "What is the sound of one hand clapping?" At first, this doesn't seem to make sense. What is the answer? But the answer is not important. The aim of the riddle is to teach your mind new ways of thinking.

SIKHISM

*"There is only one God
Whose name is Truth
The Creator
Without fear, without hate
A timeless being, not born
Self existent
Great and compassionate
Revealed only by the Guru's grace."*
(The Mul Mantar; the first words of the *Guru Granth Sahib* and a basic statement of Sikh belief.)

The founder of Sikhism, Guru Nanak, was born in Punjab, India, in 1469. Dismayed by the divisions between the two dominant religions of India - Hinduism and Islam - Guru Nanak taught a new way of thinking which stressed tolerance and equality.

Guru Nanak was the first of ten gurus, or teachers, who continued to preach the message of Sikhism. The word Sikh means "someone who learns". When the tenth guru, Gobind Singh, died in 1708, he chose the sacred scriptures, instead of a human guru, to be his successor. Called the *Guru Granth Sahib*, these are made up of hymns composed by six of the gurus and compiled by Guru Arjan.

DIVISIONS... DIVISIONS... CAN'T WE HAVE TOLERANCE AND EQUALITY FOR A CHANGE...

Sikhs believe in one God. By remembering God and helping other people, they hope to move closer to God. Everyone is believed to be equal in God's eyes. So Sikh men take the name Singh (or "Lion") and women the name Kaur (or "Princess").

In addition, devout Sikhs have five symbols of their faith. These date back to the time of the Khalsa brotherhood, founded by Guru Gobind Singh to defend the Sikh faith from persecution. They are:

The Five Ks

1. *Kesh* - uncut hair. This shows dedication to God because it is not interfering with nature.
2. *Kangha* - wooden comb. For keeping long hair clean and tidy.
3. *Kaccha* - white shorts. Worn under other clothes to show modesty and purity.
4. *Kara* - steel bracelet. This represents eternity (the bracelet) and strength (the steel).
5. *Kirpan* - sword. A reminder to Sikhs to defend the truth.

• Fact File
Numbers of Sikhs: c. 18 million
Where began: Punjab, India
Places of worship: gurdwaras ("gateways to the guru")
Sacred texts: *Guru Granth Sahib (Adi Granth)*
Major festivals: Vaisakhi; Diwali; Gurpurbs (Gurus' births and deaths and other anniversaries)

Why do we have religion?

This part of the book looks more closely at the central issues of religion. For billions of people, these play a huge part in shaping and giving meaning to their lives. But don't forget, you don't have to be religious to ask BIG QUESTIONS and expect BIG ANSWERS. These are issues which affect us all.

- WHAT IS THE MEANING OF LIFE?
- HOW WAS THE WORLD MADE?
- WHY AM I HERE?
- IS THERE A GOD?
- WHAT HAPPENS WHEN I DIE?
- WHERE DOES EVIL COME FROM?
- IF GOD IS GOOD, WHY IS THERE SUFFERING?
- WHY DO GOOD PEOPLE SUFFER?

Body and soul

One of the most important things that religion provides is a framework for people's lives, both in their everyday, physical existence and in their spiritual lives. Many religions, for example, have a moral code or a set of values according to which people can lead their lives. This code can help them decide what is right and wrong.

Religion also helps people to make sense of the world they live in, and of their place in it, and to cope with problems and difficulties as they arise. For religious people, their beliefs are a whole way of life, not just an added extra.

Some people would argue that you should take responsibility for your own actions and not rely on a set, or prescribed code to tell you what to do. They say that religion stops people thinking for themselves.

Belief or blind faith?

What do you believe?

I BELIEVE OASIS ARE THE GREATEST BAND IN THE WORLD.

That Alan Shearer is the greatest footballer?

That Nike trainers are the best thing since sliced bread?

I BELIEVE LIFE EXISTS ON MARS...

That Coke tastes better than Pepsi?

I BELIEVE IT'S TIME FOR MY DINNER—

Everyone believes in something.

IT'S TRUE BECAUSE I BELIEVE IT...

AND I BELIEVE IT BECAUSE IT'S TRUE.

All religions have beliefs but not all beliefs are religious.

Religious belief is based on accepting a set of ideas and ideals as true, even if they cannot be proved beyond a doubt. Believing in things even when you don't have proof of them means having *faith* in them.

For example: the Earth is round = PROVEN FACT, God is good = ACT OF FAITH.

Religious belief in these things has a profound effect on people's lives, affecting how they live and how they view the world.

But is it really possible to believe in something you can't see, touch or prove scientifically? That's beyond the realms of everyday experience? Or do you think that "seeing is believing", or "faith is blind"?

FAITH IS BLIND! OOPS...

How do you reach your conclusions?
Through belief in God?
Through personal experience?
Through scientific proof?

In common

Many religions have issues in common, both in terms of belief and practice. These are the basic ingredients which make up a religion, though not all religions include all of them and all religions have different ways of interpreting them.

1. Belief in God, gods or a supreme power.

2. A theory about how the world was created.

3. A moral code for its followers to live by.

4. A belief in an inner life or soul.

5. A theory about good, evil and suffering.

6. A form of worship or prayer.

7. Sacred texts or scriptures.

8. Rituals to mark special events and times in your life.

9. A theory about what happens when you die.

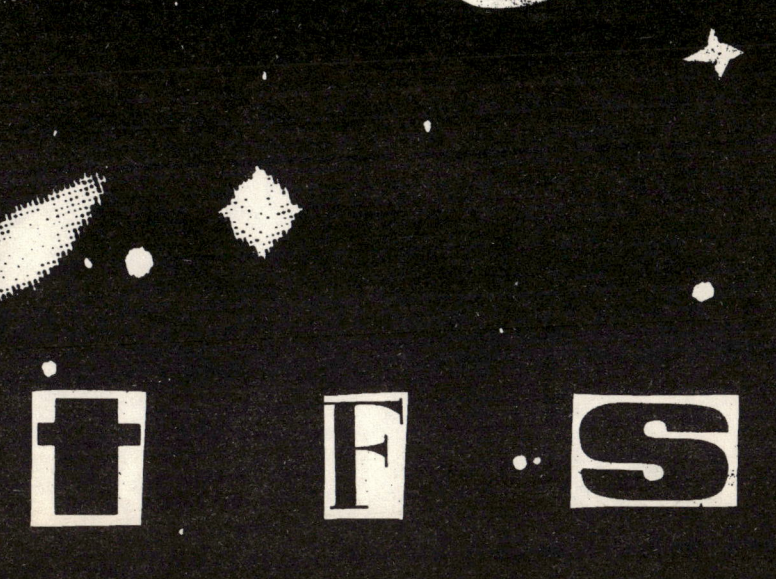

So, who is God?

Many religions believe in a supreme force, or God, which has control over the universe and human **destiny**. Living as God would wish and showing devotion to God are very important aspects in people's religious lives. They believe that, without God, life would be meaningless and there would be nothing to look forward to after death.

But what does God look like?
Where does God live?
How can you tell that God exists?
And why do people believe in God at all?

God's nowhere and everywhere...

God is a cloud...

God is a blob...

He or she?

Let's have a quick look at the first of these questions.

What does God look like?

An old man with a flowing white beard sitting on a cloud?
A shapeless blob?
An invisible gas?

Believers would say that it doesn't really matter what you think God looks like. It's how you follow God's wishes that matters.

God with a capital G

Some religions, such as Judaism, Christianity, Islam and Sikhism, believe in one God only, with a capital G. He (or indeed she) is omnipresent (everywhere), omniscient (all-knowing) and omnipotent (all-powerful). He created the world and watches over it, and is eternal and everchanging. In Christianity, God has often been described as a loving father.

Hindus worship a wide variety of gods and goddesses which represent aspects of a supreme being (Brahman, who is also sometimes referred to as God). Many of these deities are very popular in their own right. Ganesh, the elephant-headed god, for example, is worshipped at the start of any new venture – moving house, starting a new job, going on a journey – because he is the god who removes obstacles.

Buddhists do not believe in God with a capital G. The Buddha did not claim to be God nor did he want to be worshipped as such. He considered the problem of suffering too urgent for people to waste time worrying about the existence of God.

God - the great debate

So, does God really exist? Let's look at some of the arguments for and against.

YES!
- There must be good to balance all the bad in the world.
- Some people say they have felt the presence of something more powerful than themselves.
- There must be something more to life than death.
- Each person's life has meaning and purpose, given by God.
- God's existence provides the answers to life's mysteries which cannot be explained otherwise.

THE WORLD IS SO AMAZING THAT ONLY GOD COULD HAVE CREATED it.

NO!
- You can't believe in something you can't see.
- Science can explain many of the wonders attributed to God, such as creation.
- If God is so good, why does he allow famines, earthquakes and other types of suffering to happen?
- And why does he allow good people to suffer while bad people often do very well for themselves?
- Believing in God stops people having to think or act or take responsibility for themselves.

PEOPLE HAVE INVENTED GOD TO SOLVE THEIR PROBLEMS!

In the beginning

Many religions explain the creation of the world and everything in it as the work of God or a supreme power. These beliefs are expressed in creation stories, which not only tell the story of creation but also try to explain more about the world and people's place in it. Some believers interpret these stories quite literally (see page 81). But many others accept their message but not their factual accuracy. *Why* the world was created is more important than *how*.

In the Jewish and Christian religions, a story of creation appears in the first book of the Bible, Genesis.

The Seven Days of Creation

DAY 1. IN THE BEGINNING GOD CREATED THE UNIVERSE. AND SEPARATED LIGHT AND DARK TO GIVE DAY... AND NIGHT.

DAY 2. GOD MADE THE SKY AND CALLED IT HEAVEN.

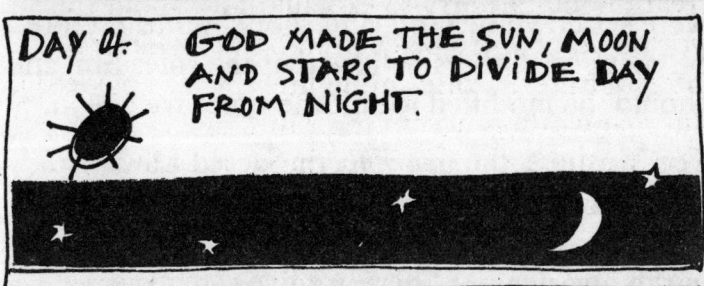

DAY 3. GOD CREATED THE DRY LANDS AND THE SEAS — HE MADE GRASS, TREES AND PLANTS.

DAY 4. GOD MADE THE SUN, MOON AND STARS TO DIVIDE DAY FROM NIGHT.

DAY 5. GOD CREATED THE BIRDS AND CREATURES OF THE SEA.

DAY 6. THEN GOD CREATED ALL THE CREATURES ON EARTH AND MADE MAN ...AND WOMAN in _HIS_ own image.

DAY 7. ZZZ GOD RESTED. HE MADE THIS A HOLY DAY ON WHICH NO WORK SHOULD BE DONE.

A code for living

Living a good life, according to God's wishes, is a crucial part of most religions. Some expect their followers to behave according to a strict set of guidelines or rules which tell them how to act in different situations. They believe that these rules were set down by God, and should not therefore be changed. Others believe that the rules can, and should, be modified to suit the times we live in.

For Muslims, the *Shari'ah*, or Sacred Law, provides a code of conduct for daily life, derived from the *Qur'an* and the *Sunnah* (Muhammad's words and deeds). There are five categories of obligation:

1. *fard* - compulsory e.g. praying five times a day; fasting during Ramadan
2. *mustahab* - recommended e.g. praying more often; showing hospitality
3. *mubah* - allowed but not encouraged e.g. going to the cinema
4. *makruh* - disliked but not forbidden e.g. smoking; divorce
5. *haram* - forbidden e.g. drinking alcohol; adultery

IJMA

So, what happens when a new law is needed for a new situation? Then the Shari'ah uses three decision making methods - *ijma*, *qiyas* and *ijtihad*. These are based on the *Qur'an* and the *Sunnah* but do not take answers directly from them.

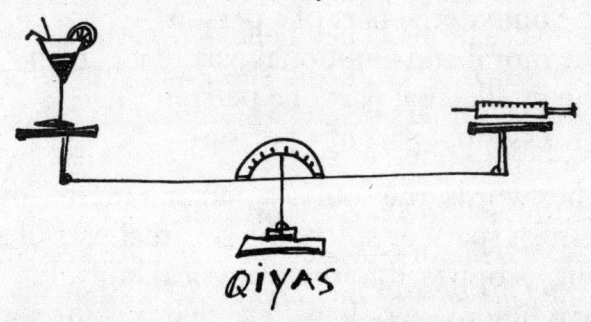

QIYAS

- *Ijma* - consensus or agreement reached after long debate by learned Muslim scholars, well versed in the *Qur'an* and *Sunnah*.
- *Qiyas* - comparing a modern problem to something similar in the *Qur'an* or *Sunnah* e.g. comparing the modern problem of drug taking to drinking alcohol (which is dealt with in the *Qur'an* and is forbidden).
- *Ijtihad* - making up your own mind in keeping with the Shari'ah.

IN KEEPING WITH THE SHARI'AH OF COURSE.

IJTIHAD

Saving your soul

What is your soul? First, here's what the dictionary says:

soul
1. The immaterial part of a person
2. The moral and emotional part of a person
3. The intellectual part of a person
4. The essential part of a person

In other words, the soul is a person's mysterious innermost spark or spirit, the spiritual part of a person, as opposed to their physical body. In many religions, people believe that it is the soul which gives life and breath to the body. But, unlike the physical body, the soul is immortal – it never dies. The ultimate aim of life, in many religions, is to merge your individual soul with God, the supreme soul.

JUST TRYING TO CATCH KITTY'S LITTLE SOUL...

Kitty R.I.P

Buddhists do not believe in an immortal soul. They believe that each person is made up of a bundle of five characteristics - the body, feeling, perception, volition (will), and consciousness. Like the parts of a bicycle, these can easily be taken apart, replaced and put back together again. So who you are is constantly changing.

Good, evil and suffering

One of the most difficult questions for religions to answer is this:

IF GOD IS SO GOOD, WHY IS THERE SO MUCH SUFFERING?

Why doesn't God use his power to prevent suffering or to relieve suffering when it happens?

Here are some possible answers:

1. Suffering happens when people turn from God towards evil.
2. God has given people **free will**, to decide for themselves how to behave. Misuse of this power can lead to suffering.
3. Some pain and suffering are necessary to bring about good. For example, you might have to suffer some pain at the dentist's to get rid of your toothache.

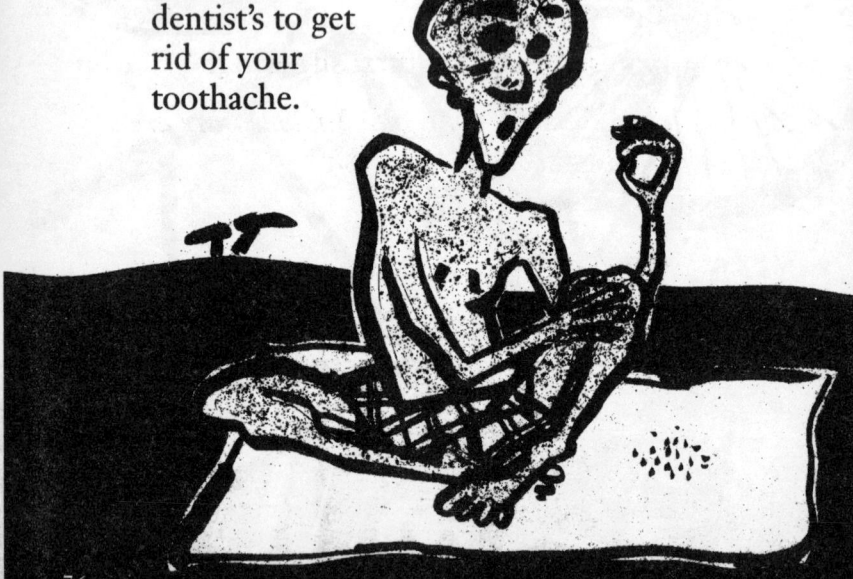

4. God must have a reason for allowing pain and suffering. But we do not know what it is.
5. God uses suffering to test people's faith.
6. Suffering is a punishment from God.

For Jews, Christians and Muslims, evil and suffering were unleashed on the world in the Garden of Eden by Adam and Eve, the first man and woman. God forbade them to eat the fruit from the tree of knowledge (of good and evil). But tempted by a serpent, they disobeyed God's orders and were banished from paradise as punishment.

Hindus believe that suffering happens as a result of the law of karma (the law of cause and effect). Bad actions in a previous life cause suffering in this one. The way out of suffering is to lead a good life and move closer to moksha or **liberation**.

Yes, but what about earthquakes? And floods? And famines? Why are innocent people often the ones to suffer the most? Is there a difference between man-made and natural suffering?

"From the beginning of time, pain and pleasure are written in man's fate by the Creator."
(Sikh Guru Granth Sahib)

The power of prayer

- *Why do people pray?*

In many religions, prayer is a means of communicating with God and of establishing a closer relationship. Prayer may be part of a set service, or of group worship. Or it may be a private, personal act.

- *What do people pray for?*

Prayer often consists of giving thanks or praise, or asking for help, or forgiveness. It helps people to express their deepest hopes and fears. Some prayer consists of reciting passages from the sacred texts, or just sitting and listening.

- *How do people pray?*

There are many ways of offering prayers - in words, songs, gestures or in silence. Some people use prayer-beads to help them concentrate as they pray. They repeat the same prayer over and over again, as they count off the beads.

- **What do religious leaders do?**

Priests, ministers, monks, rabbis, imams and pandits are some of the religious leaders and teachers within different religious communities. They offer prayers and gifts to God on behalf of the worshippers, guide worshippers in matters of faith and try to explain difficult religious concepts or ideas.

"Blessed are you, Lord our God, King of the universe, in whose world there is nothing lacking, and who has provided it with good creatures and beautiful trees to give delight to the children of men."
(Jewish prayer)

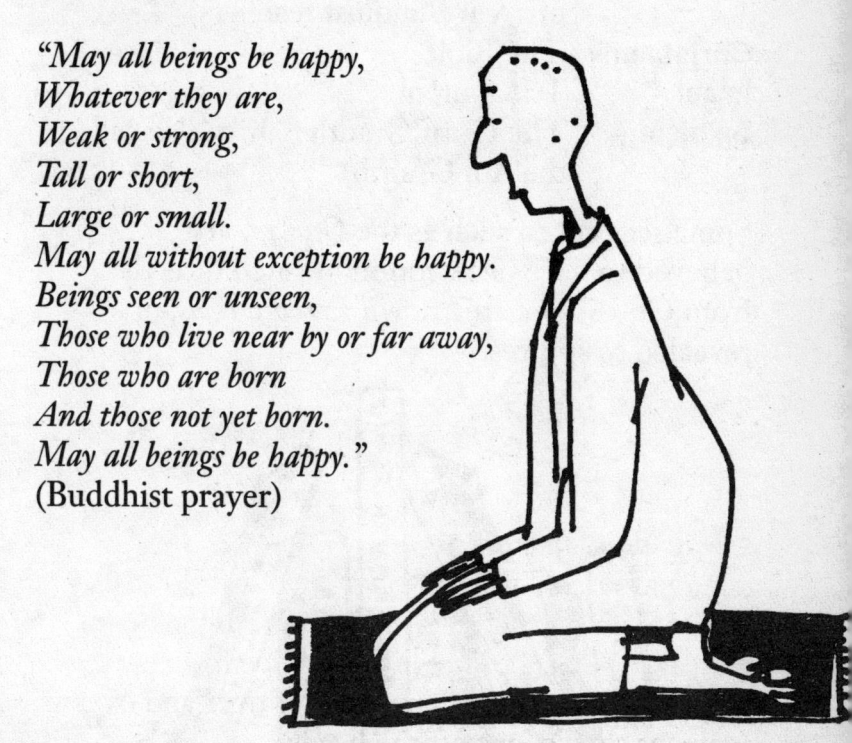

*"May all beings be happy,
Whatever they are,
Weak or strong,
Tall or short,
Large or small.
May all without exception be happy.
Beings seen or unseen,
Those who live near by or far away,
Those who are born
And those not yet born.
May all beings be happy."*
(Buddhist prayer)

Sacred texts

Each of the major religions has its own sacred texts, or scriptures, which tell people about God and give guidance about how they should live. (Buddhist scriptures are different, dealing with the life and example of the Buddha, rather than God.) These texts are treated with great respect and reverence.

Hinduism - Vedas; Upanishads; Ramayana; Mahabharata
Judaism - Tenakh (Hebrew Bible); Torah (first five books of the Tenakh); Talmud
Buddhism - Tipitaka (Three Baskets); Diamond Sutra and other sutras (also the works of great Buddhist teachers)
Christianity - The Bible
Islam - The Qur'an
Sikhism - The Guru Granth Sahib (also called the Adi Granth)

Some scriptures, such as the *Qur'an*, are believed to have been communicated directly from God. They are known as *revelations*, or revealed scriptures.

Literal or Liberal?

The way in which the sacred texts are interpreted is a source of great debate and discussion. Many use stories and myths to get across complicated thoughts, teaching and ideas. So how should they be understood? Literally? Or liberally?

People who interpret sacred texts LITERALLY believe that every word comes directly from God, was accurately recorded and cannot, therefore, be changed. They are also called fundamentalists.

People who interpret sacred texts LIBERALLY believe that, while every word was inspired by God, they were also affected by the historical times they were written in and by the individual views of their authors. They should, therefore, be interpreted differently today, to suit the modern world we live in.

THE WORD OF GOD CANNOT BE CHANGED!

GET REAL! THIS IS THE 20th. CENTURY.

Rites and rituals

- **rite** A required or usual procedure or action in a religious or solemn ceremony or observance; a body of usages characteristic of a religion
- **ritual** Of, with, involving religious rites; a prescribed order of performing a religious service

In most religions, special ceremonies are held to celebrate key events in the religion's history (such as the birth or death of significant figures), key events in nature (such as the coming of spring) and key events in a person's life (such as birth, reaching adulthood, marriage and death).

In Sikhism, a new-born baby is taken to the gurdwara to be blessed and named. The *Guru Granth Sahib* is opened at random and the top hymn of the left-hand page read out to the parents. The baby's name must begin with the first letter of the first word of this hymn.

YES I KNOW it's NEITHER A RITE NOR A RITUAL BUT it's NICE —

82

These key times are remembered with feasts, fasts, festivals and special events which aim to bring people together to give thanks or help them through times of change. Rites and rituals also help people to cope with difficult times in their lives, such as the death of a loved one.

In some religions, performing such ceremonies is also seen as a way of gaining approval from God or the supreme power. In ancient times, keeping the gods happy was considered crucial in averting disaster, such as a bad harvest or a drought.

But some people reject the whole notion of organised religion and all the paraphernalia - the ceremonies, prayers, rites and rituals and all that goes with it. They believe that people should be able to structure their own lives, by themselves.

What happens when I die?

The belief that death is not the end is central to many religions. So how do they answer the biggest, and most mysterious, question of all - what happens when I die?

In some religions, such as Hinduism, your soul is believed to be reborn, or reincarnated, in another body - plant, animal or human - when you die. According to the law of karma, the quality of your next rebirth depends on how well or badly you have lived in the past. The ultimate aim of life is to be liberated from this cycle of events and attain moksha where your soul becomes one with Brahman, the supreme soul.

In Buddhism, the aim is to work towards *nirvana*, a state in which all unhappiness and suffering ceases.

Heaven and Hell

Christians believe that Christ rose from the dead and ascended (rose) into heaven to be with God. Heaven is often described as a paradise, or state of bliss, which follows death. So, death is not the end but the start of a new life with God.

And if you haven't towed the line? Well, you could end up in Hell, a terrible place traditionally full of fire and demons where the wicked and sinful go after death. Not that you'd actually burn in Hell. Heaven and Hell are more states of mind than actual places, designed to keep people on the right track.

Muslims believe that, when you die, your body remains in the grave until the Last Day, or Day of Judgement. Then Allah will judge everyone, living and dead, and send them to Heaven or Hell depending on their past deeds and actions.

"Hell is other people."
(Jean-Paul Sartre, French philosopher)

In religion's name

Alongside the issues which different religions have in common are their many different views and opinions which have, throughout history, often been a source of conflict. When these difficulties are found in communities facing other problems - for example struggles for political power, economic problems such as unemployment and poverty, arguments which have been around for many years and never properly resolved - the cocktail can be lethal.

It's often the religious differences, rather than the similarities and points of agreement, which hit the headlines, and the other sources of conflict are overlooked.

WAR IN BOSNIA

In 1992, war broke out Bosnia (part of the form Yugoslavia) between th country's different ethni communities. The situatio was made worse by conflic between different religiou groups.

MUSLIMS AND HINDUS CLASH

In 1990, fighting broke out between Hindus and Muslims in Ayodhya, India, over a mosque said to be built on the site of the birthplace of the god Rama, one of the most important and best-loved gods of Hinduism. The Muslims also claimed it as a holy place.

IN THE NAME

> **PEACE BREAKS DOWN IN PALESTINE**
> Since the formation of the state of Israel in 1948 in the ancient land of Palestine, there has been constant conflict between Israel's Jewish population and the mainly Muslim Palestinian Arabs.

Even within the same religion, different attitudes and points of view can lead to conflict.

> **TROUBLES IN NORTHERN IRELAND**
> Deep-rooted conflict between the largely pro-British Protestant community and the largely pro-Irish Catholics has led to years of violence and bloodshed in Ireland and Britain.

But how do religions match war and conflict with their teachings on peace, harmony and the value of human life? Or, given human nature, are such conflicts always likely to happen? Can such conflicts *ever* be justified?

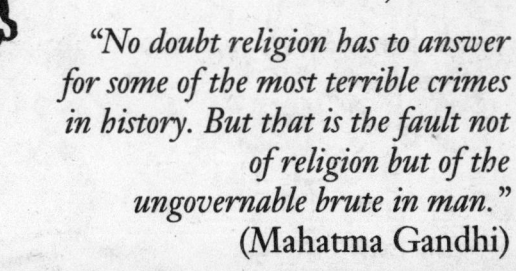

"No doubt religion has to answer for some of the most terrible crimes in history. But that is the fault not of religion but of the ungovernable brute in man."
(Mahatma Gandhi)

Spreading the word

Some people also argue that religion has caused conflict wherever it has tried to convert others to its own cause.

When the Spanish conquistadors (conquerors) reached Central and South America in the 16th century, they saw nothing wrong in forcibly converting the local Aztec and Inca people to Christianity, nor in claiming their lands "in God's name".

"In Gold's name" would have been more appropriate since it was greed for gold which led them so far afield.

In the 18th and 19th centuries, European Christian **missionaries** began their work in Africa and Asia. Missionary-explorers, including David Livingstone, combined the spreading of religious ideas with exploring the interior of Africa, much of which was completely unknown to Europeans.

While many missionaries did important pioneering work in medicine and education, their reforming zeal often did great damage to traditional societies and their cultures. After all, the whole point of being a missionary was to wean people away from their existing, and in the missionaries' opinion, misguided, beliefs.

Conflict in daily life

Closer to home, conflict can also arise in our multi-faith society. One challenge is the tension between a person's religious values and the demands of modern, Western society. For example, only recently have Sikh motorcyclists been made exempt from having to wear crash helmets, simply impossible whilst wearing a turban. Before this, they could be charged with breaking the law. Which do you think is the right solution? What else could have been done?

"Being a Buddhist in Britain is not easy. There's a huge gulf between the 'give me more' attitude of Western society and the Buddhist teaching that the way to end suffering is to extinguish greed and desire."
(Western Buddhist)

Life can get very difficult if you're trying to follow your own religious beliefs and yet keep in with your friends, who might want to do things differently. For example, Hindu and Muslim girls are not encouraged to choose their own boyfriends. Their marriages are usually arranged by their parents, and other boy-girl relationships are sometimes frowned on. But what do you do if all your non-Hindu or non-Muslim friends talk about is boys?

And what would happen if you wanted to marry someone of another faith? Would this cause problems?

How people cope with these tensions depends how strongly they feel about their religion and culture and how great is the social pressure for them to conform and be like everyone else.

New religions ...

> THERE ARE ALSO SOME BRAND-NEW RELIGIONS IN THE WORLD.

The long-established major faiths have billions of followers all over the world. But new, smaller religious groups continue to emerge. Some develop and remain within an established religion. Others break away to become independent religions in their own right. There are also some brand-new religions, with new ways of looking at the world.

For example...

Rastafarianism

Rastafarianism was founded in the 1930s, in Jamaica, West Indies, when Marcus Garvey predicted the coming of a black messiah in Africa. Ras ("Prince") Tafari, who became Emperor Haile Selassie of Ethiopia in 1930, was hailed as this messiah. Rastafarian beliefs are based on biblical teachings, mixed with African traditions. They believe that, one day, they will return to freedom in Africa from exile in the countries where their ancestors were taken as slaves.

Reggae music, in praise of Jah (God), is a very important part of Rastafarian worship. In the song "Forever loving Jah" for example, the famous musician Bob Marley sings of how Jah helps people cast away their fears.

Hare Krishna

The Hare Krishna Movement, or International Society for Krishna Consciousness (ISKON), was founded in 1966 by a Hindu holy man, Bhaktivedanta Swami Prabhupada. Based on devotion to the god Krishna, the movement gained thousands of followers in the West. Many were attracted by its teaching of giving up attachment to material things and concentrating instead on achieving greater inner peace and self-awareness. Worshippers show their devotion by chanting the names of Krishna and Rama.

... and non religions

People who do not follow a religion still face the same BIG questions about life. How do they answer them? Some don't bother. Others base their answers on a non-religious view of the world.

Humanism

Humanists believe that human beings have the power within *themselves* to make sense of life and to live in the world, based on belief in science, reason and human experience, rather than in God. They believe that the *human* qualities of caring and cooperation should be used to make life better for everyone, rather than relying on the supernatural. Your fate is in your own hands!

OR to put it simply: MAN IS THE MEASURE OF ALL THINGS. — PROTAGORAS

WHAT ABOUT ALIENS, MATE?

The golden rule of humanism is to treat other people as you would wish to be treated yourself. A sentiment shared by all religions.

Q: What is an agnostic?

A: Agnostics say that, since there is no proof, it is impossible to know if God exists or not. They would believe in God if it could be proved that God exists. The word agnostic comes from the Greek for "not knowing".

Q: What is an atheist?

A: An atheist is someone who categorically does not believe in the existence of God. The word atheist comes from the Greek for "not God".

Sects and cults

While many new religious groups are widely accepted, some can provoke greater controversy. These groups are known as *sects* and *cults*.

Strictly speaking...
... a **sect** is a group which breaks away from its parent church (usually an established religion).
... a **cult** is a new religious group with a new, often charismatic, leader and a new set of rites and rituals.

All the world's major, established religions started off as sects or cults. But some modern sects and cults are seen as having strange or sinister customs and practices which many people frown on.

Some people condemn these groups for preying on young or vulnerable people and playing on their feelings of disillusionment or insecurity by offering them the chance to belong to a group and to put meaning into their lives. Sects and cults are blamed for brainwashing new recruits, through hypnosis. Some followers become so dependant on the group that they will do whatever they are told, to the extent of breaking all ties with their families, committing crimes and even of taking their own lives.

Of course, there are exceptions to every rule. Sometimes the criticism is unfair and misleading.

In March 1997, 39 members of the Heaven's Gate cult were found dead in their headquarters in San Diego, California, USA. They had committed suicide. An extremely high-tech organisation, the group had posted a farewell message on its World Wide Web site. This explained that the group wanted to leave their earthly bodies in order to join a spaceship trailing the Hale-Bopp comet. The appearance of the comet was the signal they had been waiting for.

So, when is a cult not a religion? One of the key things is a cult's insistence on secrecy. Religions declare their beliefs openly, in their sacred texts and services. Anyone who can accept these beliefs is welcome to join the religion. Cults, however, rely on secret knowledge revealed to followers only by the cult's founder. It is not open to all. Followers are required to isolate themselves from the world, and may even face threats to their families if they do not exactly follow the rules. This allows them to be exploited (used) by the cult and its leader. The leader's power and character are all important. When the leader dies, so, often, does the cult.

The challenge of science

Do scientists believe in God?

If they do, how do they square the supernatural aspect of religion with scientific knowledge and reason?

Does such knowledge destroy belief?

For many centuries, particularly in Europe, the Christian church was extremely powerful, the source of all wisdom about God, the universe and everything. Science was fine as long as it backed up the church's teachings.

But there were problems...

For hundreds of years, scientists believed that the Earth lay at the centre of the universe, and that the Sun, Moon and planets travelled around it. This reinforced the church's teaching that the Earth lay at the centre of God's creation, as the Bible said it did.

But in the 17th century, an Italian scientist and astronomer, Galileo Galilei, made a series of startling discoveries. His work supported an earlier theory put forward by Nicolaus Copernicus, a Polish priest. Both came to the same conclusion - that the Sun, not the Earth, lay at the centre of God's universe and that the Earth was only one of several planets orbiting the Sun.

For daring to express views which contradicted the Church's teachings, Galileo was brought before the Inquisition, the church court responsible for trying people accused of **heresy** (anti-church views), in Rome and forced to renounce his beliefs. He was only pardoned by the Vatican (the headquarters of the Roman Catholic Church) in 1992!

Act of God or Big Bang?

In 1656, an Irish archbishop, James Ussher, announced that the Earth was created on Saturday, 3 October 4004 BCE, at 10 a.m. precisely. He based this date on information found in the Bible.

In fact, scientists now think that the Earth formed 4,600 million years ago. The first living things appeared some 3,200 million years ago and the first humans about 2 million years ago. They believe that the universe itself formed some 15,000 million years ago, in a gigantic explosion called the *Big Bang*. This blasted vast amounts of matter and energy out into space where they formed the Sun, stars, moons and planets.

And how did human beings come to be? In his startling new theory of evolution, the 19th-century British scientist, Charles Darwin, stated that humans were descended from apes and were not created by God, as previously thought.

These scientific views seem to contradict the accounts of creation found in the world's religions. Or were these religious interpretations intended not as scientific theory but simply as an illustration of God's amazing power and as an explanation of what could not, at that time, be explained by science?

Many religious people would argue that it is perfectly possible to believe both versions. Both are evidence of God's grand design for the universe; God could have caused the Big Bang and started the process of evolution.

- People who believe that the world was created by God, exactly as the Book of Genesis says, are called *Creationists*.

- People who believe that the world was formed by the Big Bang are called *Evolutionists*.

Playing God?

Thanks to amazing breakthroughs in technology, the boundaries of scientific research and knowledge are being pushed further and further outwards. Today, scientists can do all sorts of things previously unheard of, like putting men on the Moon, curing some forms of cancer, replacing people's hearts and lungs when they prove faulty, and more.

But just how far should modern science and medicine go without being accused of playing God?

Take the following dilemmas:

1) Should scientists intervene in order to create life by artificial means, for example, by using IVF (*in vitro* fertilisation) to produce "test-tube" babies?

    - **NO** - babies should only be created naturally, as God intended.
    - **YES** - life is precious and valuable however it's created.

2) Should scientists intervene in allowing extremely sick people, such as victims of PVS (persistent vegetative state), to die?

    - **NO** - life is sacred and no one but God has the right to take it away.
    - **YES** - people have a right to die if there is no hope whatever of them having quality of life.

3) Should scientists be allowed to use genetic engineering to alter the genetic make-up of animals? (Genetic engineering means the biological technique used to move genes from one species to another to speed up growth, alter shape and size, and even create brand-new species.)

- **NO** - it's unnatural. God created animals and they should not be tampered with.

- **YES** - under strict controls, genetic engineering can be used to produce new medicines, better quality food and, possibly, organs for transplanting into sick humans.

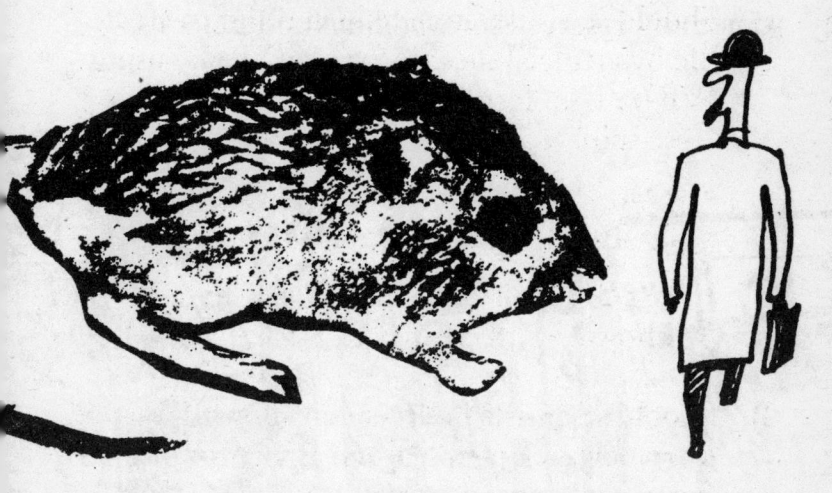

What would your response be to these dilemmas? Could you answer **YES**, yet still believe in God?

(Of course, you could answer **NO** and not believe in God - just believe that tampering with the natural order of things might do long-term damage we can't yet predict.)

THE FUTURE OF RELIGION

Is religion alive and well?
How will it fare in the 21st century?
Will more people turn towards or away from religion as the pressures of modern life increase?
Does religion still have a place?

As well as answering the BIG questions of life, religion must also be prepared to question itself.

It is true that in some parts of the world, religion is generally thought to be on the wane.
For example, for many people brought up as Christians in Britain, going to church is now something reserved for weddings and funerals.

In other places, however, such as Africa, Christianity is becoming ever more popular, with churches and congregations flourishing. In fact, throughout the world, religious groups of all kinds are mostly in excellent health.

Has Church attendance dropped in Britain because money and possessions have become the new religion? Has money become a substitute God? Or sport? Or pop music? Or shopping? Have supermarkets and football stadia become the new churches?

Or have people simply found different ways of expressing their religious beliefs – ways that can't easily be measured, such as worshipping at home?

Or have they turned to different religions altogether? Certainly Buddhism, for example, is currently attracting more and more followers in Britain.

Secular versus sacred

The word *secular* means being concerned with worldly matters and not with religious or sacred affairs. Secular countries do not have an official state religion (although many were organised along religious lines in the past). Nor do they teach a particular religion in schools (e.g. in assemblies).

This can lead to conflict in countries where the majority of people follow a particular religion.

In Turkey, for example, the vast majority of people are Muslim. But, in the 1920s, under the leadership of Kemal Ataturk (1881-1938), Islam ceased to be the state religion. Today, however, the growth of the country's Islamic groups poses a threat to Turkey's secular status, with the government split between supporters of the pro-Islamic Welfare party and the secular True Path party.

One of the secularists' key demands is a banning of any propaganda for *Shar'ia* (Muslim sacred law) on TV or radio.

In other parts of the Muslim world, too, fundamentalism – sticking strictly to teachings prescribed by a religion – is on the increase. In 1979, a fundamentalist Islamic revolution came to power in Iran, under the leadership of Ayatollah Khomeini. Since then, Iran has been ruled by Muslim law. In Algeria, the Islamic Salvation Front (FIS) has been very successful in recent elections.

The West says that fundamentalism threatens peace and international relations. The fundamentalists argue that all they want is a return to Muslim social and religious values which they feel have been harmed by the influence of Western culture and high-handedness.

It's often the Islamic fundamentalists that hit the headlines, but of course *all* religions have fundamentalists.

Getting the message across

If religion is to survive into the 21st century, some people argue that it simply has to move with the times. And if this involves using high-tech means, so be it.

> Don't be square. Check out the 3D tour of Noah's Ark only on the World Wide Web!

For some Christian groups in the USA, **evangelism**, that is, telling others about what you believe, is already big business, using millions of computers, fleets of cars and aircraft, television and radio stations (with millions of listeners) and publishing millions of books and pamphlets each year, to spread its message. During some church services, the image of the preacher is projected on to a giant screen for all to see.

In Britain, the Church of England has launched a glossy TV advertising campaign to spread its message.

The Internet has got in on the act, too. You can get all sorts of information about religious groups on the World Wide Web. Even the Vatican has opened its own site at http://www.vatican.va You can find out about the Roman Catholic Church and there's even a tour of some of the Vatican's world famous paintings.

OF COURSE, NOT EVERYONE APPROVES...

Facing future problems

The issues and problems facing the world's religions have changed over time and will continue to change, as people and society change.

What are the main problems to be faced in the future?

And how will they be tackled?

1. The role of women
• Many religions are now debating the role of women, who have traditionally been excluded from some religious activities. The Church of England has recently allowed women to become priests. **Traditionalists**, however, still argue that women cannot become priests. In strict Muslim countries, such as Saudi Arabia, women have to wear traditional robes and veils, as a way of keeping with the *Qur'an*'s requirement of modest dress. In other countries, such as Syria, the rules are more relaxed and women are allowed much greater freedom.

2. Abortion
• Most religions believe that life is a special gift from God and should be treated with care and respect. If abortion means taking life then it should not be allowed. The question is at what point does human life begin, at birth or at conception? If the answer is at birth, then abortion does not mean that a life has been taken. Tricky! Some people argue that a woman has a right to choose what happens to her body, and that it is better to have an abortion than to bring an unwanted child into the world.

3. Contraception
• With the world's population rapidly outgrowing the world's resources, many religions are having to take another look at whether or not to accept the use of contraception. Even if religious teaching does allow their use, people are sometimes reluctant to use contraceptives. Some people traditionally view large families as an insurance for the future and some are worried that if they don't have many children, their future will be very bleak and lonely.

4. Euthanasia
• At present, **euthanasia** is illegal in Britain and many other countries. But should terminally ill people be helped to die, if that is what they themselves wish to happen? Or does the sanctity of life argument overrule their wishes? Most religions believe it does. Yet, would God really want people to suffer unnecessarily?

5. World poverty
- All religions have a teaching on helping those less fortunate than themselves. Some have set up organisations which aim to help people to help themselves. Christian Aid, for example, now works in over seventy countries worldwide. Some religions have fixed rules about charity. In Islam, giving money to those in need is known as *zakat*, one of the Five Pillars of Islam. In a world where the rich seem to be getting richer, and the poor, poorer, these teachings have an ever-more valuable part to play.

6. The environment
- Many religions agree that, as God created the natural world and everything in it, it is our duty to look after it. Unfortunately, the major culprits in the destruction of the environment are its human caretakers. A change of attitude is needed and fast, with people taking far greater responsibility for the world they live in.

Faith to faith

Many people hope that the future lies in greater communication and cooperation between the different faiths. Many say that this is the *only* way in which religion as a whole can face the future.

The World Council of Churches, for example, was formed in 1948 to encourage different Christian groups to work more closely together. This process of cooperation is called the **ecumenical**, or "worldwide", movement.

Many other multifaith groups exist, for example, the Inter-faith Network for the UK. They work for greater understanding between the different faiths in the hope that this will lead to greater mutual acceptance and understanding.

So, the future of religion lies in all our hands, whether we believe in a particular faith or not. Whether religion will survive and flourish remains to be seen. Perhaps its future lies in greater involvement in global problems, using its influence for worldwide good? Or perhaps it can become part of a much wider range of views and ideas, both religious and otherwise, concentrating more on what they have in common rather than on their differences.

But remember, whatever you believe...

*"The road to good is the roughest and steepest in the universe.
It is a wonder that so many succeed, no wonder that so many fail. Character has to be established through a thousand stumbles."*
(Swami Vivekananda)

Good luck

Further Reading

A Lion Handbook: The World's Religions
(Lion Publishing 1982; reprinted 1991)

Religions: A study course for GCSE
by Alan Brown, John Rankin and Angela Wood
(Longman 1988; reprinted 1995)

Thinking about God
by Maureen Harrison and Sharon Kippax
(HarperCollins 1996)

Religion and Life
by Victor W. Watton (Hodder & Stoughton 1996)

Guidelines for life
by Mel Thompson (Hodder & Stoughton 1990)

World Faiths: Buddhism; Christianity; Islam; Judaism; Hinduism; Sikhism
(Teach Yourself series) (Hodder & Stoughton)

World Religions
by John Bowker (Dorling Kindersley 1997)

Atlas of Holy Places and Sacred Sites
by Colin Wilson (Dorling Kindersley 1996)

Out of the Ark: Stories from World Religions
by Anita Ganeri (Macdonald Young Books 1994)

The Usborne Book of World Religions
by Susan Meredith (Usborne Publishing 1995)

Who's Who in World Religion

Abraham The leader of the first Jews about 4,000 years ago, who entered into the covenant (agreement) with God. As a supreme act of faith, Abraham offered the life of his only son, Isaac, to God. Isaac was saved before the sacrifice was made.

Allah The Arabic word for God. Muslims believe that the will of Allah was revealed to the prophet, Muhammad. This was later written down as the *Qur'an*, the Muslims' sacred book.

Amaterasu-Omikami The main spirit, or kami, in the ancient Shinto religion of Japan. Amaterasu-Omikami is the sun goddess, from whom the Japanese imperial family claimed to be descended.

Amitabha Buddha The heavenly Buddha worshipped in Japan and China. He is believed to live in a "pure land" far to the west where faithful followers go when they die.

Brahma One of the three most important Hindu gods, Brahma is worshipped as the creator of the universe.

Brahman The supreme being, or soul, of Hinduism. The aim of a Hindu's life is to merge their own, individual soul with that of Brahman.

Confucius Also known as K'ung Fu Tzu. A Chinese thinker and teacher whose philosophy of life influences Chinese society to the present day. Famous for his *Analects*, or sayings.

Guru Gobind Singh The tenth guru, or teacher, of the Sikhs. As his successor, he appointed the Sikh sacred book, the *Guru Granth Sahib*, instead of a human teacher.

Guru Nanak The first guru, or teacher, of the Sikh religion. He preached belief in one God and emphasised that everyone was equal in God's eyes.

Jesus The teacher, preacher and prophet of Christianity. He is worshipped as the son of God, and as the Messiah, or anointed one, whose coming was foretold by the ancient scriptures. Jesus was crucified on a cross but is said to have risen from the dead before rejoining God in heaven.

Krishna An extremely popular Hindu god, Krishna was the eighth avatar, or appearance, of the god, Vishnu. Although born a prince, he was brought up as a cowherd. He is the main character of the *Bhagavad Gita*, one of the most sacred books of Hinduism.

Lao Tzu A Chinese thinker who taught a philosophy called the Tao, or "way". He was lived at the same time as Confucius.

Mahavira Jains follow the teachings of Mahavira, who lived at the same time as the Buddha in India. Like the Buddha, he left home at the age of about 30 to live as a monk.

Moses Moses became the leader of the Jews and led them out of captivity in Egypt to the Promised Land of Israel. He received the Torah and the Ten Commandments from God on Mount Sinai.

Muhammad The final prophet of Islam who received Allah's holy will for the world later written down as the *Qur'an*.

Rama The seventh avatar, or appearance, of Krishna, Rama is immensely popular in Hinduism. His exploits in love and war are told in the *Ramayana*, one of Hinduism's most sacred books.

Shiva One of the three most important Hindu gods. Shiva is worshipped as the destroyer and re-creator of the universe.

Siddhartha Gautama The Indian nobleman who became the Buddha, or enlightened one. He taught people to follow a "middle path" between the two extremes of luxury and hardship.

Vishnu One of the three most important Hindu gods. Vishnu is worshipped as the preserver, or protector, of the universe. He appears on Earth from time to time, as an avatar, to save the world from disaster.

Zoroaster A prophet who lived and taught in ancient Persia. His teachings concentrated on the struggle between good and evil, represented by two great gods.

Key Dates in World Religion

c. 20,000 BCE Statues of female figures suggest a mother goddess cult.

c. 15,000 BCE Prehistoric hunters paint animals on the walls of the Lascaux Caves, France.

8,000-6,000 BCE The Megalithic Age in Europe.

c. 3,000 BCE The Mesopotamians (in ancient Iraq) build ziggurats to honour their gods.

c. 3,000-30 BCE The Ancient Egyptians mummify their dead to preserve their souls in the afterlife.

c. 2,500 BCE The Indus Valley Civilisation flourishes in north-west India. Its beliefs form the basis of Hinduism.

c. 2,000 BCE The Jewish religion begins in the Middle East.

c. 1250 BCE Moses leads the Jews out of slavery in Egypt (the "Exodus").

c. 750-30 BCE The Ancient Greeks worship the great gods of Olympus, ruled over by Zeus.

6th century BCE Life of Mahavira, the teacher of Jainism in India. Suggested date for the life of Zoroaster (although experts differ widely on these dates).

551 BCE Birth of K'ung Fu-tzu, better known as Confucius. Lao Tzu, the teacher of Taoism, lived at about the same time.

c. 563-483 BCE Life of Siddhartha Gautama, the Buddha.

2nd century BCE The Romans conquer Greece and "adopt" many of the Greek deities.

1st century CE Life of Jesus.

570-632 CE Life of Muhammad, the prophet of Islam.

8th-11th centuries CE The Vikings flourish in northern Europe.

13th century CE Zen and Pure Land Buddhism reach Japan.

c. 1325-1521 CE The Aztecs of Mexico make human sacrifices to the god of the Sun.

1469 CE Birth of Guru Nanak, the first guru, or teacher, of the Sikh religion.

1930s CE Rastafarianism begins in Jamaica, West Indies.

1966 CE The Hare Krishna Movement begins in India. It soon gains many thousands of followers in the West.

Glossary

Avatar Literally means "one who descends". In Hinduism, the god Vishnu appeared on Earth ten times to save the world from disaster. These appearances are called avatars. The most famous are the gods, Rama and Krishna. Vishnu also appeared as a fish, a tortoise, a boar and a lion.

Blasphemy To talk about, or treat, the beliefs, deities or sacred objects of a religion in a disrespectful or impolite manner.

Destiny Believing in destiny means believing that events in your own life, or in life in general, will follow a predetermined path. You may be able to influence your destiny by behaving in a particular way, or you may have no control over it whatsoever.

Ecumenical Ecumenical means "worldwide" and is used to refer to the movement encouraging the various Christian churches to work more closely together. The focus of the ecumenical movement is the World Council of Churches which was set up in 1948.

Euthanasia The bringing about of the gentle death of a person who is suffering from a painful and incurable illness.

Evangelism The practice of spreading the Christian Gospel which puts an emphasis on proclaiming and sharing God's love for the world, as revealed in Jesus Christ.

Free will The choice people have about how to think and act, whether well or badly, and the responsibility they have for their own thoughts and actions.

Fundamentalism Believing that the rules and scriptures of a religion should be very strictly followed and not be interpreted or changed in any way.

Heresy An opinion or practice which goes against the normally accepted teachings of a religious body.

Immortal In many religions, the gods are believed to be immortal, that is, have the power to live for ever, never growing old.

Karma The law of cause and effect which forms an essential part of Hindu and Buddhist beliefs. Karma means being judged by your actions, good or bad, and the results of those actions, good or bad. Karma also means acting selflessly, without thought for your own reward.

Liberation In some religions, such as Hinduism, liberation means finally breaking free from the endless cycle of birth and rebirth, and becoming one with God.

Missionaries People who try to spread their own religious beliefs among followers of a different faith. Both Buddhism and Christianity were spread throughout the world largely as a result of missionary activity.

Persecution Throughout history, people from different faiths have been picked on and badly treated, even killed, because of their religious beliefs.

Pilgrimage A journey to a holy place, which might be a shrine or tomb, or a natural feature, such as a sacred river or mountain. A pilgrimage may be undertaken to remember a past event, to earn merit, give thanks, ask for a favour or to make amends for doing something wrong.

Reincarnation The belief that, when you die, your soul lives on and is reborn in another body which can be human, plant or animal. This means that you live a series of lives, not just one life. Reincarnation is also called rebirth.

Shaman In the spirit religions of Africa, North and South America, and Australia, the shaman acts as a go-between between the world of the spirits and the people. While the shaman is in a deep trance, contact is made with the spirit-world to ask the spirits for favours, such as good hunting or cures for sickness.

Soul Many religions believe that people are made up not only of their physical bodies, but also of an invisible, innermost spark or spirit, called the soul. This is thought to live on after a person's physical body has died.

Spiritual To do with the spirit or the soul. The word spiritual is often used simply to mean "religious" or "divine".

Traditionalists People who believe that the traditional rules and teachings of a religion, for example, as they are presented in the scriptures, should be strictly followed and not tampered with or changed.

INDEX

abortion	114	evangelism	113
Abraham	34	evolution	103, 104
afterlife	20, 21, 84	Exodus	35
agnostics	95	festivals	7, 33, 37, 41, 47, 49, 53, 57, 83
ahimsa (non violence)	42		
Allah	50, 51, 85		
Ancient Egyptians	20-21	Five Ks	57
Ancient Greeks	22-23	Five Pillars of Islam	52-53
atheists	95	Four Noble Truths	39
Aztecs	26-27, 88	free will	76
Bhagavad Gita	33	fundamentalists	81, 111
Bible	7, 49, 70	Galilei, Galileo	101
blasphemy	47	Gandhi, Mahatma	9
Brahma	32-33	Ganesh	67
Brahman	31, 67, 84	Garden of Eden	77
Buddha	38, 40, 41, 42, 67	God	8, 10, 34, 47, 57, 61, 64-65, 66-67, 68-69, 74, 76, 77
Buddhism	13, 37-41, 55, 84, 109		
Buddhists	38-41, 42, 67, 75, 90		
Christ	46, 84	goddesses	
Christianity	13, 46-49, 66, 70, 88, 100-101, 108, 116	Hindu	32-33, 67
		mother	17
		of the Sun	54
		gods	15
Christians	13, 46-49, 77, 84, 89, 108	Ancient Greek	22-23
		Hindu	32-33, 67
		Mesopotamian	19
churches	7, 49	of nature	14
common issues	62-63	Roman	22-23
conflicts	6, 86-87, 90	Sun gods	26
Confucius	44	gurdwaras	12, 57, 82
contraception	115	Guru Gobind Singh	56, 57
covenant	34, 35	Guru Granth Sahib	56, 57, 77, 82
creation of the world	24, 29, 70-71, 102-105	Guru Nanak	56
		gurus	56
crucifixion	47	Hare Krishna Movement	93
cults	96-99		
Day of Judgement	85	Heaven	19, 43, 84
Dhammapada	38, 41	Hell	43, 84
dharma	30, 40-41	Hinduism	13, 30-33, 56, 67, 84
Diamond Sutra	41		
ecumenical movement	117	Hindus	12, 30-33, 42, 77, 90
Einstein, Albert	9		
enlightenment	38, 55	Holocaust	37
environment	116	Holy Spirit	47
euthanasia	115	Humanism	94

Indus Valley Civilisation	30	Rastafarianism	93
Islam	13, 50-53, 56, 66, 116	reincarnation	33, 42, 84
		religious beliefs	10, 11, 15, 17-18, 59, 60-61
Israel	34, 37, 47		
Jainism	42	religious leaders	79
Jesus	46, 47, 48	revelations	51, 80
Jews	34-37, 77	rites and rituals	15, 82-83
Judaism	13, 34-37, 66, 70	Romans	22-23, 46
		sacred cow	12
kami	54	sacred fire	43
karma	33, 42, 77, 84	sacred texts	80-81
		science and religion	100-107
King, Martin Luther	9	sects	96-99
Krishna	32, 93	Shari'ah	72-73, 110
Lao Tzu	44-45	Shaw, George Bernard	9
Mahavira	42	Shinto	54-55
Makkah (Mecca)	50, 51, 52	Shiva	32-33
mandirs (temples)	12, 33	shrines	18, 41
Marx, Karl	9	Siddhartha Gautama	38
meditation	38, 55	Sikhism	13, 56-57, 82
megaliths	18		
Mesopotamians	19	Sikhs	12, 56, 57
Messiah	46	sins	47
missionaries	89	soul	20, 33, 74-75
moksha	33, 77, 84		
monks	8, 38	spirituality	10
Moses	34-35	spirit worship	28-29
mosques	6, 7, 12, 53	stupas	41
		synagogues	6, 7, 37
Muhammad	50-52	Talmud	37
multifaith society	12, 90-91	Taoism	45
Muslims	12, 50-53, 72, 77, 85, 90, 110, 111	Tao Te Ching	45
		Tenakh	37
		Ten Commandments	35, 36
		Tipitaka	41
nirvana	84	Torah	37
Noble Eightfold Path	39, 40		
nuns	8	Upanishads	31, 33
Parsis	43	Vatican	101, 103
persecution	37, 57	Vedas	33
pilgrimages	53	viharas	41
poverty	116	Vikings	24-25
prayer	52, 78-79, 83	Vishnu	32-33
		Vivekananda, Swami	33, 118
Promised Land	34	Wesak	41
Qur'an	50-51, 53, 72, 73	women (role of)	114
		World Council of Churches	117
Rama	32, 86, 93		
Ramadan	51, 53	Zoroaster	43
Ramayana	33	Zoroastrianism	43